IN SEARCH OF THE

WINNING SYSTEM

Published in 2013 by Raceform Ltd
High Street, Compton, Newbury, Berkshire, RG20 6NL

A catalogue record for this book is available from the British Library.

ISBN 978-1-908216-95-3

Cover illustration by Loz Taylor (www.loztaylor.com)
Designed by Fiona Pike
Printed and bound by the CPI Group (UK) Ltd, Croydon CR0 4YY

IN SEARCH OF THE

WINNING SYSTEM

Peter May

Acknowledgements

I would like to thank everyone who has had an input to this book at the various stages of development especially those who have contributed directly to my racing and computing knowledge. Most specifically Nigel, John, Miles, Graham and close family members with a keen interest in the sport, as well as the "Forster Boys" for all the information about training and preparing racehorses. Also, at the proofing stage, my thanks go to Sara, Rhianna, Nathan, Andy, Tony, and Marilyn who all spotted typing errors and more importantly encouraged me to leave in the biographical detail and not just write "another horseracing book". Finally I'd like to thank Mike who could have rewritten this in a much more entertaining style but would probably have left out anything remotely mathematical.

Contents

Chapter One

The Most Reliable Way to Make a Profit

Systems are an integral part of betting. Whether it is football, horseracing, casino games or the National Lottery, if there's money bet on the outcome of an event then someone somewhere will have a system which, it will no doubt be claimed, is guaranteed to make a profit. This has been the case for thousands of years since the first dice were rolled or the fate of two gladiators facing each other across the blood-stained sand of the Colosseum was debated. But it was not until the 17th century that systematic approaches to gambling were subject to rigorous mathematical analysis, mainly through the work of Jerome Cardan, Blaise Pascal and Pierre de Fermat. Though based on games of chance, most notably those using dice, this research evolved into the theory of probability, one of the key branches of mathematics and the basis for all betting.

In the modern era the wide-spread proliferation of personal computers and the availability of sporting data have made it much easier for racing enthusiasts to develop their own betting systems. Potentially profitable ideas and mere hunches, the value of which remained unknown previously, can now be put to the test at home and validated against an accurate set of historical data. This has led to a better awareness of the relationships between the key racing factors and the outcome of races, putting the bettor in a much stronger position from which to formulate a winning strategy. Using horseracing data to inform decisions and design a well structured, systematic approach to betting remains the most reliable way to return a long-term profit from the sport.

Not every bettor would necessarily agree with this, and a great many firmly believe that systems are the poor relation of *value betting* and the more conventional approaches to solving the *racing problem*. However these apparently diverse methods have much in common and it can be argued that everyone who bets on horses uses a systematic approach to a greater or lesser extent. An analyst who studies the form and bases all decisions purely on information gleaned from historical races and statistical relationships may feel that a system would not form even the smallest part of the method.

But consider this conventional approach to race analysis: the form is analysed, ratings checked, previous race times studied, suitability of the race conditions determined, strength of the race in terms of the opposition evaluated, along with running styles and the likely pace or lack of it. These conclusions are combined into a price, a figure believed to represent the chance of success for each, or a selected number, of the runners. The final step in the process determines whether a bet will be made or not and essentially concerns the following test:

> If the price available is greater than the calculated value price then back the horse.

But isn't that a system? An *if... then...* rule, in this case featuring just one condition, is the definition of a system. Whether the bet is made or not is determined by this rule. If the condition is met the bet is placed, otherwise it isn't. Some may claim that the calculation of the value price is not systematic since it is based purely on judgement of the facts, and the mere application of a rule at the very final stage of the process does not constitute a system. This is a reasonable view.

However, the process of determining a value price concerns making evaluations based on the data relating to each horse. These assessments can only be made by the application of rules learned over many years of betting. Without the in-depth knowledge these connections provide, it is simply not possible to draw any meaningful conclusions about a race. For instance, when discussing a bet a race analyst who adopts a non-systematic approach might say, "I like it when jockey x rides for stable z", or "I don't like small horses around this big track". These are connections which have been distilled from historical race results. For the system user these rules will normally be the direct outcome of data analysis; for conventional bettors they are probably due to assimilation, by noticing the patterns as they occur and mentally recording them.

Both rule identification approaches are valid providing

they have been established in a logical, precise fashion. My preference, and that of the system player, is for the former. It is possible to be more confident about the validity of the rule if the data supporting it can be checked and analysed. But the outcome is the same for both learning techniques: a set of rules which forms a knowledge base that can be used in the analysis of future races.

For many bettors their reluctance to use systems is due in part to the perceived simplicity of such techniques. It is difficult to see how a rule with perhaps just two conditions could outperform a detailed analysis of a race involving all available information. However it is important to remember that a system is not designed to predict the race winner, but instead is attempting to identify a small region of the market where the chance of success is not fully accounted for by the prices on offer.

Therefore some rules can be simplistic in their form and still produce profitable returns. For instance many of my most profitable systems have had very few conditions, specifically those based on the draw bias. For certain tracks the rule would simply state that all horses running from a particular stall over a certain distance should be backed. The reason these methods worked so well had nothing to do with the accuracy with which they determined the chance of success. Their effectiveness was due to the fact that a critical factor, the stall allocation, had not been fully taken into consideration by those setting the prices, and therefore presented an ideal opportunity for making a profit.

The advantages of using systems over conventional race analysis methods are due to their consistency and unambiguous form. A system or rule can be applied just as well today as it can tomorrow. However, the analysis of a race can differ depending on the way the analyst views the event. This is due to the subjective nature of race analysis. A conclusion determined from a set of results today may not agree with one derived from an identical set of data some months ago.

These changes may be a result of the performance of recent selections. It is easy for an analyst to change a method, perhaps unknowingly, if experiencing a particularly good or poor run. Over confidence, or lack of confidence, can play an important role in the analysis of a race and consequently remove any degree of consistency over an extended period of time. The outcome of a system is not subject to these influences and the determination of a qualifier will remain the same regardless of recent events.

Naturally there are many poor systems available, such as those advertised in the racing press and on the internet. These only serve to reinforce the view amongst non-system users that such approaches are destined to fail. Take the following example which was advertised on a website purporting to provide top-quality racing systems:

> The Logic System is based on the fact that around 33 per cent of all horse races are won by the favourite. If

> you bet on six races a day, logic dictates that you'll win two out of six. To succeed with this system you just need to pick one horse winner a day. Buy a racing newspaper or use the internet. Find a meeting with six races or more. In each race, stake just two per cent of your bank on the favourite. With a bank of $250, you'd stake $5 and the aim would be to win $5 (so you bet $5, and get $10 back, including your stake). You must only bet on the favourite horse if the odds are 11/8 or better. For those unfamiliar with odds, just divide the first figure by the second. So, 11/8 is 11 divided by eight, which is 1.375. Now, if you find that the odds on a particular horse are less than 1.375, forget about it, wait for the next race.
>
> When you have a winner, quit for the day, otherwise bet again. Use the following staking plan – 1-1-2-4-8-16. That means, with a bank of $250, you bet two per cent ($5) multiplied by the staking plan figure, which is $5 (5x1) on the first race. If it loses, bet $5 (5x1) on the second race, if that loses bet $10 (5x2) on the third, $20 (5x4) on the fourth, $40 (5x8) on the fifth and finally $80 (5x16) on the sixth. If the sixth race loses, quit for the day. It is HIGHLY unlikely you'll go for six races without the favourite horse winning.

This is a prime example of a poor system that will not return a profit. The claim that 33 per cent of races are won by the favourite is reasonably accurate, however those favourites that start at 11/8 or longer win at a rate of only one in four, 25 per cent, a statistic which is conveniently ignored. Furthermore, the claim that, "It is highly unlikely you'll go for six races without the favourite horse winning" is also inaccurate. In fact the chance of no winning favourites priced at 11/8 or longer in a run of six races is 18 per cent, almost one in five.

Finally the staking plan is guaranteed to increase losses. The variable approach has no logical reasoning to support it: increasing the stake because the previous bet failed is only going to increase losses. In fact during 2011 backing all the favourites priced at 11/8 or more to level stakes would have lost 6p/£, adopting the suggested staking plan more than doubles the loss to 13p/£. Fortunately not all systems are like this one. A rigorously researched method which has been thoroughly tested on an unbiased set of results can become a very profitable addition to the bettor's range of techniques.

While I use conventional race analysis methods from time to time, the majority of my betting is systems based. Consequently I have spent many years searching for rules which are capable of beating the book and returning a long-term profit. The following sections detail this search, the lessons I have learned along the way, and a selection of the systems I have unearthed.

Chapter Two

What's in a Name?

Doubtless, many an historian could make a cogent case that 1968 was a critical year in the 20th century: the first manned Apollo spacecraft orbited the moon; two charismatic world leaders were assassinated and Britain's first super group *Cream* was on the verge of break-up. But the hallmark of the 12 months from my rather immature perspective was the formulation of my very first betting system, and one which I eagerly applied to that year's Grand National. Foinavon had won the previous year's race in dramatic circumstances (a fact not entirely digested by this fairly raw recruit to the racing world) and many bettors were thinking twice about speculating in a contest which could produce such unpredictable outcomes. My "system" was oblivious to these events though and for the 1968 race the selection was Red Alligator. I watched the race through half screwed-up eyes and fingers fully crossed and after for me what was a world-changing nine-and-a-half minutes of racing drama, the 100/7 shot hurtled home first. The system was one-from-one.

The following year the method singled out Highland Wedding, a lightly-weighted 12-year-old trained by Toby Balding in Hampshire, who memorably took just 0.8 seconds longer than Red Alligator to win the race from Steel Bridge. My method was two-from-two but more importantly I had enough money for a new elastic-band-powered balsa-wood aeroplane, a handful of Airfix models and enough bait to keep me happily perched on the river bank for the rest of the season.

At this point I ought to add, for those who were beginning to wonder, that I did not of course place the bets myself. Even had the law been in my favour, I'd still have been far too short in stature to make my presence known above the office counter. Instead, my grandfather acted as "runner" while I waited outside Sam Cowan's LBO in Ock Street, Abingdon, taking in the somewhat sickly smells emanating from the Morland brewery, sited just a few yards away between the town's main thoroughfare and the river who gave its name to that same road.

The brewery was a permanent fixture in Abingdon from the 1860s until its purchase and eventual closure by Greene King at the start of the new millennium. Its earthy odours would regularly envelop the streets with that familiar stirring blend of malt, yeast and hops, which to this day still evoke in me such strong recollections of my earliest acquaintance with the noble art of betting.

Sadly, these nostalgic pleasures are no longer to be savoured in Abingdon. The sensory diet nowadays is strictly limited to a rather unedifying concoction of petrol and diesel fumes from the vehicles which clog this main traffic artery as they pass slowly through the market town. Paradoxically, while my grandfather would never let me enter a betting shop, he was certainly not averse to buying me half a pint of the local brew when we often spent a summer's evening at the pub, mulling over the essentials of the day such as where we would catch the most fish. It was a strange contradiction which I found difficult to rationalise at the time but one that I particularly welcomed nonetheless.

So, how had I formulated such a remarkable system? Had I spent many hours trawling through the formbook and seeking out the key patterns which would inform my decision? Did I have a string of contacts in the main stables plying me with key information on how the runners had performed on the gallops? Had I found an exceptionally lucky pin and gleefully stuck it in all the right places? No, it was simpler than that. To a boy just a few weeks off his fifth birthday, writhing reptiles in glutinous swamps are a serious draw, so Red Alligator was an obvious choice.

In 1969 the daughter of a close neighbour was to be married on National day, so Highland Wedding qualified under that unfailing rule which states that the banker bet is always the one with the most relevant name at the time. Needless to say, as the years unfolded, I did encounter some loopholes in this allegedly cast-iron approach and discovered, to my cost, that it wouldn't in fact yield the level of profit I'd originally come to expect. However, these formative experiences alone had achieved something much more significant, for now I was officially hooked on the sport and even more completely seduced by the allure of betting.

Ever since these first successes the National has always

entertained for me a special appeal, whether I have had a personal vested interest or not. Over the years, I have analysed the race in many different ways, some admittedly more productive than others. My current preference is to adopt a race-profiling approach. For the main races of the season, such as the Grand National and the Derby, race trends in the form of ten-year or 20-year analyses are very popular. If these races retain the same key attributes from one year to the next, the trends highlighted by these summaries can be very informative.

Unfortunately, in recent years, there have been many changes to the sport, and in some cases to the individual races themselves, which render the results from such historically proven approaches less helpful. The earlier races in the ten- or 20-year period become far less relevant, and omitting these from the data simply reduces the sample size making any conclusions much less reliable. In these cases, it is often beneficial to take a broader sample from all races which exhibit the same key attributes of the contest under review and formulate the analysis on this significantly larger, and more recent, data set. The Grand National, for instance, is a stamina-sapping class 1 handicap chase run in the spring. These key facts can be used to form a data set of all similar races which can then be analysed.

Taking as a whole all the long distance (3m3f or further) top-class handicap chases run in recent seasons, it can be shown that eight- and nine-year-old runners accounted for nearly half of all victories, with the nine-year-olds returning a 21p/£ profit at off-time exchange prices from 366 bets. Furthermore, the 518 runners carrying at least 11-00 won 48 per cent of contests and made an impressive 47p/£ profit. Analysing the runners' recent form shows that a good winning run is not entirely necessary; almost a third of winners had just one success from their last ten starts over jumps, and these returned a profit of 36p/£. However the best horses to follow are those following on from a win. The 295 runners who had been successful on their latest jumps start, took 35 per cent of long-distance handicaps, making a profit of 25p/£, with those runners that achieved a wide margin of success in the race immediately prior (ten lengths or more) able to produce a 39p/£ profit.

Using these trends to inform racehorse selection can be helpful, but they do not constitute systems in themselves, merely serving to highlight historically profitable patterns. While it is possible to find worthwhile betting methods by mining the data in this way, an ultimately more reliable system tends to be rooted in an initially plausible idea. The data then becomes a tool to verify its profitability.

During my school years the frequency with which I placed bets used to vary. They often needed to be squeezed into moments unoccupied by my other main pastimes. These primarily included playing cricket for a local league side and fishing, an activity to which I was dedicated with an almost professional zeal. However, the prospect of a bet continued to tantalise me and I modified my methods to incorporate the opinions of the *Daily Mirror*'s top tipster, as well as those of his counterpart in the *Oxford Mail*. The rationale underpinning this particular approach was that if the tipsters were broadly in agreement, and other factors coincided also, then the horse was worth my serious consideration.

Eventually, I came to the conclusion that I had been attempting to find the solution to the wrong problem. Specifically I had allowed myself to become consumed by wondering which horse was most likely to win the race. Although I had a method that was useful for finding short-priced winners, it was not one that isolated good-value bets. Predictably enough, these fairly naïve approaches of my earliest years didn't prove to be too lucrative as time wore on, but I was gaining in the sort of knowledge which would lead to my gradual realisation of an altogether more sophisticated method at a slightly later stage of my betting apprenticeship.

At school, mathematics was the only academic subject I enjoyed until I reached my O-level years when computer studies was introduced into the syllabus. It was available as a CSE and was definitely an option I was keen to pursue. In 1977 computing was a relatively novel area of study in schools and none of the teaching staff at Faringdon School (an establishment whose reputation had hitherto hinged on its success in teaching Pam Ayres how to write funny rhymes) were particularly qualified to take the subject. As a result, the class seemed to be somewhat randomly assigned to a

Mr Eric Dale, a lost soul on the face of it whose lessons would customarily end with the words, "Right, now I'm off to learn what I need to teach you next week!"

Unlike a significant minority of the staff who seemed to consider teaching a group of former secondary modern pupils as an especially unwelcome chore, Mr Dale (along with mathematician John Warwick and English teacher Marilyn Tasker as memory serves) was keen to make the time spent in the classroom as stimulating as possible, even if that meant abandoning the conventional style. Mr Dale was a lively character who brought into play some pleasingly alternative methods. Looking back it's hard to describe just what he did or didn't do but the net result was that he made me feel he cared about his pupils and their enjoyment of the lessons. I appreciated his varied and relaxed style of teaching and immediately took to computer studies which joined mathematics, woodwork and PE as the only lessons I used to genuinely savour.

In those days personal computers were simply not available, so in lessons we started by coding programs in C.E.S.I.L., a language which had in total just 14 instructions, but one which could be compiled and run on our behalf at other institutions. Once we had mastered this we were encouraged to graduate to BASIC, variations of which are still widely employed today.

To create an actual program it had first to be written in long-hand, then "carded up". At the back of the classroom were stored big boxes of punched cards which were individually labelled with instructions. We were taught to painstakingly search the boxes for the cards that matched the instructions in our programs then elastic-band them together to preserve their order which, of course, was critical. These batches of cards were then posted to Southampton University where a "card reader" would transfer the code into a mainframe computer. The following week a print-out would be returned to school with the output from the program, which quite often read, "Run Time Error at line ..." normally caused by cards being placed in the wrong order. However on more memorable occasions the output would list no errors and present the results of a perfectly working piece of code.

This process of getting the program from the classroom to the computer was far from ideal as well as very time consuming, but at that time there were no other practical options and, for a group of students who had never seen a computer before starting the course, it felt like we were sitting proudly in the very front row seats of a technological revolution.

I do recall that my eventual completion of a prototype program designed to simulate a simple fruit machine provided me with a quiet sense of deep satisfaction, and although I only gained a Grade 2 in the examination (mainly because I had to leave early that day in order to catch the bus home), I knew that computing was an area I would always find captivating.

Following these searching examinations and a further couple of weeks' welcome respite, fishing the lakes and rivers of rural Oxfordshire, I followed my father's footsteps and started working for a local building firm as a carpenter's apprentice. I was not the only new recruit. Since my inaugural visit coincided with the start of the summer vacation, our workforce was suddenly swollen by the unexpected addition of a number of Oxford University students. Though based in Abingdon, our work was located at Kidlington which necessitated a 40-minute daily trip inside an uncomfortably clunking van. It did at least afford us the time to talk (in work's time on the way, but in our time on the return journey) about various topics.

On one particular morning a student employee asked me why I had opted so quickly for paid employment as opposed to the idea of taking an academic tour through further education. I merely replied that I had not even considered it as an option due to the expense. The truth was, (and I know this will sound remarkable in this day and age) that I was wholly unaware that state school pupils were even entitled to attend university. The student then explained the process to me in no uncertain terms: "Just get a couple of A-levels, which are really easy, then go to university. It won't cost you anything; in fact you will get paid to go."

This came as a real shock to me since I had convinced myself that universities were privately owned institutions that charged inordinate fees for students to prepare for working life thereafter. At first, I remember not believing this preposterous claim, far too good to be true did it sound to me. So I approached another young member of our team to have the vicious rumour fully confirmed. He also added that I might prefer to choose to study a single subject.

This convinced me that the university route was a feasible direction for me. I enjoyed woodwork and carpentry, as I do even now, and the 50p per hour I was earning was still useful in keeping my Suzuki moped roadworthy, but I preferred mathematics, and I was strongly attracted to the notion of those long, lazy summer days between term-times, perched on the edge of sun-drenched ponds packed full of roach, tench and bream. All of a sudden it all seemed quite irresistible. So after completing just a few, meagre weeks of my apprenticeship I deserted the idea completely and returned to school with a fresh sense of purpose.

I often think back nervously to those few weeks and the immeasurable difference they made to my life. Fate, as ever, certainly played its part. Had I been taken on by a different company then I would never have met those particular students and in all probability would never have been diverted along the path I finally chose. Had I delayed my start with the company until the end of August, I would never have met any students at all and my career might very well have been a very different story of assembling roofs and second-fixing houses, perhaps alongside my cousin who is one of the most skilled carpenter's in the county – poles apart from computer programming and horseracing that's absorbed me ever since.

It still surprises me to think how apparently minor decisions taken or apparently trivial comments made by one individual, or by people only remotely connected to that individual, can affect a person's entire future. Maybe Edward Lorenz was correct when he asserted that a butterfly's flight in one continent could cause a tornado in another.

Unfortunately computer studies was not available at A-Level, so I opted to take mathematics and further mathematics both of which comprised pure mathematics and statistics. It was a fairly strict diet but one I knew I would enjoy.

Two years later I was offered a place at Westminster College, Oxford, to study for a Bachelor of Education (Honours) degree in mathematics which, if I were to succeed, would give me qualified teacher status. It was soon after my arrival at the college that my true passion in life was about to be properly launched, once and for all. Unfortunately, racing was not one of the "three Rs" educationalists had in mind, and betting was not due to feature prominently any time soon in Tory plans for a National Curriculum. Yet, it was the sport of kings that now began to strengthen its engrossing grip around my ambitions.

As a Methodist college, the sale of alcohol on campus was strictly prohibited. It had no bar. In fact, even public consumption of inebriating liqueurs anywhere on site risked serious censure. Traditional values with a capital "T" were upheld (as best they possibly could manage). Fortunately, there were no such restrictions on my betting inclinations, though I did try to keep these as private as possible just in case the rector felt obliged to dispense some suitably solemn advice. No, it didn't take long in my first year for me to organise a Grand National sweepstake which turned out to be very popular with fellow students if a little less so with the select staff whose discretion I warily trusted. I also became a regular attendee at the local Tote office. I was most surely broadening my own education, though its links to the B. Ed. I was meant to be aiming for were, at best, tenuous.

While at Westminster I combined my studies with a part-time job in a local hotel, The Rose Revived at Newbridge. As well as having two restaurants and a bar area, the hotel provided quite comfortable accommodation for up to 20 residents. It was also very expensive but, in general, the people who used the "Rose" could easily afford the inflated prices; money was not an issue for most of them and it was not uncommon to see the occasional Rolls Royce pull up alongside the odd Bentley in the car park.

One morning, while I was preparing the bar area, one of our regular residents, a tall, tweed-suited man in his late fifties who was rarely known to smile on purpose, asked if he could use the telephone. I explained how pleased we would be to assist and duly sent him in the right direction. Once connected, he began by uttering the intriguing words, "Ten pound Carson Yankee". I immediately tuned in with all the subtlety I could muster, listening intently while he listed four race times. Hastily, I scribbled these down on a pad. My morning session was due to end at 2.30, so I decided I would drive home as quickly as possible and check the racing results throughout the afternoon (which in those days followed the news on Radio 2). Willie Carson did indeed have a very special afternoon. All four of his horses led the rest home and the £121 stake (which included the tax) had returned a profit well into four figures. It was one of those early, more significant successes which most underlined for me, the absolute love I was developing for what I seemed to be able to do best. And it made me want more.

When I returned for the evening session the lucky punter and his wife were seated in the bar area enjoying a pre-meal drink. I say "enjoying the drink" but it was hard to tell. They were certainly not celebrating the big win with any obvious semblance of joy, choosing instead to inscrutably inspect their respective newspapers, avoiding all but the most essential communication. Eventually, he slowly lowered his copy of *The Telegraph* and mumbled something to his wife. She wearily shook her head by way of reply. He came over to the bar and ordered a single Campari. In spite of his miserable manner I was bursting to lock him into some sort of exchange about racing. Evidently, here was an astute gambler who had just the type of skills I wanted to gain. In the end, I had to resist because he would then have known I'd eavesdropped on his telephone call, a fact he may not have entirely appreciated. I have a vivid recollection of what followed.

After I had prepared his drink he put a 50p piece on the edge of the bar. He then put his forefinger on the coin and pushed it halfway across the polished wood surface and released it. On returning from the till with his change, I found that he'd gone, so I dutifully placed the 2p piece beside the drink that still remained. On returning, he picked up his drink, put his finger on the two pence coin and slid it across the bar in the same fashion he had the original payment. "That's for you," he said. I looked at the shiny, copper coin in momentary disbelief, then back at him. Not even the merest flicker of a smile crossed his sullen face. He was deadly sincere. The 2p was a tip. I thought back to his telephone call and reflected on the winnings I knew he'd made. Even his stake was more than I would get paid for ten days (100 hours) of work. I just had to smile. I had no wish to make him feel any more superior than he did already. And as if to make a small point that the sum was not an overly generous one, I just had time to drop the coin into the charity box before he turned away.

In hindsight, though, the episode did teach me two things: one, that serious winners always take money seriously, no matter what the amount; and secondly, that I swore never to be so arrogant myself with another human being. I hope I've kept that promise, no matter how much I've ever won or lost.

Mind you, his bet did make me wonder if I might one day emulate his achievements and enjoy similar wins. This is a normal reaction when confronted with others' success which is why National Lottery winners are paraded by the media in front of an envious public and why bookmakers regularly publicise any large payouts. There is no better advertisement for gambling than the ostentatious celebration of winning punters, whether their moment of truth was born of the pin, pure panic, or a perfected method of bet selection months or more in the making.

Clearly the aloof hotel resident's approach was systems-based and the outcomes on the day were indeed excellent, but the overall worth of his system cannot be so certainly assumed. It's possible to justify selecting runners from the same stable when the trainer's recent strike rate appears to show that his runners are generally performing well. A stable in good form is often worth noting, mainly because it suggests that the horses are completely virus-free and the training regime has honed them to peak fitness. But I remain unconvinced that the same level of expectation could ever be sensibly applied to a jockey. Did Carson, for example, have days or weeks when he was riding more skilfully than at other times? Obviously he would have good runs where his win rate would improve, but this was surely due to the form of the stables for which he was riding. I can see how this could potentially have increased his confidence, but remain unsure that this would have actually improved his riding performance significantly.

Restricting a bet of this type to a single jockey's rides makes the assumption that this rider will be on the four best-value bets of the day. For me, that seems unlikely, though those of you who were on Frankie Dettori at Ascot in September 1996 may disagree. Consequently, I decided that I would prefer to either select from the entire card, restrict the bets to a single stable or even to a sire whose progeny may be suited by the prevailing conditions. I concluded quite quickly that the single jockey approach was at best dubious, and, at worst, deeply flawed.

I wasn't completely convinced about the virtues of the "Yankee" itself either. Multiple bets of this type do inflate returns for positive methods, but also exaggerate the losses for losing systems. More importantly, though, this bet restricts the placement to a single bookmaker which means that it's not always possible to secure the best prices about each of the selections. Resultantly, the overall profit margin is reduced. And although I did play Yankees for a couple of years it is no longer a bet I would consider.

In my second year at Westminster I got into the habit of attending race meetings with a small group of friends, including a petite, dark-haired girl called Sara who also happened to share my penchant for mathematics. To this day, I'm still fathoming whether it was the fences and the formulas or the equestrian and the equations which made us such an irresistible combination. Either way, this fellow student agreed some years later to become my wife, an event all the more remarkable given her thorough insight into the risky nature of some of my investment activities. Having said as much, it's probably just as well that her eyes were forced so wide from the outset. It must have prepared her well for much of what was to follow.

Our first race meeting, excluding the largely less memorable Lockinge point-to-point, was the Oaks at Epsom in June 1984 where we smuggled ample refreshments in a large wicker basket so as to dodge the exorbitant on-course prices. At the time it seemed quite daring to such raw race-goers but we were poor students after all!

The day was an unqualified success in every way and augured well for our future lives wrapped up together as they would be in this other world we both loved to inhabit. We were fortunate to see the greatest flat jockey of all time, Lester Piggott, win yet another classic on a horse that I gladly had the foresight to back, Circus Plume. Also "The Shoe" had made the trip across the Atlantic and provided us with a second winner by getting Royal Racecourse over the line first in the Ashtead Stakes later in the afternoon. It was a classic day in more ways than one, and only served to deepen my fascination for the sport.

The B.Ed. course at Westminster was split "two plus two", which meant that in the first two years students focussed almost exclusively on their main subject, whereas in years three and four, all were destined to cover other school-related subjects alongside short, sharp periods of actual practice, confronted by actual, live pupils in actual, real-life settings. So, after two very enjoyable years devoting my academic energies avidly towards mathematics, my course was to radically change direction towards educational matters relating to philosophy, psychology, sociology and teaching practice itself – hardly a prospect to savour from any angle as far as I could make out.

It wasn't long before I had decided that teaching was not for me and that I was not for teaching. It has never been a decision I've had cause to question since either. Instead, I quickly determined to continue studying maths for as long as possible. At the time, my reasons were more instinctive than methodical but I always had a sense that it would lead to something concrete, even though I had little notion what exactly that something would entail.

My only sensible option, if I were to stay local and close enough to Sara, was to join Oxford Polytechnic and commit to a course covering mathematics, statistics and computer studies. This trio would provide me with the central pillars of knowledge and understanding that would enable me later to convert my favourite hobby into a bona fide career plan, though I hadn't fully realised the association at that particular point in the proceedings.

After a couple of years of complex analysis, differential equations and computer programming, I gratefully graduated with a 2.1 in December 1985 and was initially pleased to join the ranks of the full-time employed almost at once in the guise of assistant statistician at the Potato Marketing Board (PMB). My remit at the PMB consisted of writing computer programs in BASIC, FORTRAN and COBOL, as well as processing large amounts of strictly potato-related data on mainframe and micro-computers. I had never before given the world of potatoes nearly as much attention but soon my professional life was pivoting on the fluctuating markets of a singular root vegetable – and, for those who might doubt the fact, it was a surprisingly serious business.

Forecasting was a key element of the department's role and we had to determine, as far as two years in advance, the tonnage of potatoes that Great Britain would import, export, consume, waste, and produce. Once this balance sheet was constructed we then predicted the potato yield per hectare so that we could set the area required to be grown by producers in order to meet the forecast requirement. This meant that, if the forecasts were accurate, there would neither be an over-supply resulting in low farm prices requiring intervention, nor an under-supply resulting in a shortage of the crop and excessively high consumer prices.

It was of key importance to the government that we produced accurate forecasts although we were always at the mercy of the British weather, whose vagaries would regularly upset our best predictions to a greater or lesser degree. These additional, unpredictable, factors are utterly dreaded by the system player in any sphere of betting. Though they may seem inconsequential, even relatively minor alterations to the environment in which a system operates, they may have a serious impact on its performance and in many cases render it totally redundant.

If at all possible, being aware in advance of such changes and their likely effect is a critical requirement of the system player if he or she is to make a consistent profit from a systematic approach to betting. This will certainly be a recurring theme within the pages that follow, though not (I must reassure you) with the tedious frequency of the Channel 4 racing commercial breaks which are virtually making the programme unwatchable. It is though a concept worth revisiting just enough, I hope, to underline its vital significance to anyone intent on using betting systems.

For many of the larger farms and potato processors, the futures' market was guaranteed to play an important role. Buying and selling contracts on the exchange meant that these companies could hedge against future price moves. Consequently they were interested in our predictions though, of course, we were not allowed to discuss unpublished data with any organisation outside the PMB and government. This did sometimes add a little spice to the proceedings where the creation of crop reports were concerned, and we would often take phone calls from farmers and statisticians from large commercial organisations, all eager for information in advance.

Though none of the forecasting methods we used were directly applicable to horseracing, I was constantly improving my computing skills and statistical knowledge through both our own work and via visits to statistics departments in other organisations. During one Cambridgeshire sojourn to Masterfoods (a division of Mars), I became party to a substantial amount of "inside" information about their forecasting procedures and company history. I remember also departing that day as the proud possessor of a large box of extremely inviting samples, some of which turned out to be rather more tasty than others, but it was a nice touch nonetheless.

However, the real sweetener for this visitor was to have been treated to an in-depth explanation of how Mars forecasts the production of cocoa beans. As well as the usual statistical methods we all employed, Mars would go several steps further. In their efforts to create the perfect forecasting model Mars would commission aerial photographs of the cocoa crop at different points during the growing season. I queried whether this was cost-effective and was assured that it was. In order to produce the best model, Mars considered it necessary to incorporate as much data as possible and would spend thousands of pounds collecting information which would only make a minimal difference to the overall forecasting ability of the system they used.

For bettors aiming to create accurate price tissues, this tip from one of the world's largest companies should not be dismissed lightly. The models should include as much data as possible, especially data which is not generally considered. For horseracing this might mean factors relating to how a horse moved to post, or behaved in the paddock and at the post, for the current or previous races. Such data is not easy to collect with a high degree of accuracy so, in theory at least, should have more merit than the more generally available information if it is handled correctly.

In October 1986, just nine months after starting work, I was moved into the office next door and became head of statistics. The promotion meant a respectable salary rise (£7,500 to £10,200 for those interested in this type of data) but, more importantly, it promised the tantalising prospect of a private office which could only be accessed via the outer office where I had previously been operating alongside a clerk. For the type of extracurricular tasks I had in mind a spot of inconspicuous isolation was most welcome. Furthermore, I was now entitled to a comfortable chair – a never-to-be underestimated bonus in the potato industry at any time.

At the PMB in the 1980s, everyone laboured under a whole raft of rules governing office furniture and respective décor. The Statistics Department Clerk (Viv when I joined and Jeanette when I left) was a grade four, which entitled her to an unenviable basic chair, without arms or reclining facility. As assistant statistician I was graded as a seven, so I was granted access to the relative comfort of a leather-clad chair with wooden arms, but fixed legs which crucially denies its user the kind of spontaneity of movement that any alert thinker surely requires. In fact this hardwood-backed chair was very uncomfortable which was why I spent so much time in front of the computer terminal because the chair there was much more ergonomically suitable.

Further distress for some was caused by the quite woeful inadequacy of the flooring arrangements. Since the most senior employee in the outer office was only a grade seven, it meant that the floor could not be fully carpeted (three-quarters covered was the best we could hope for) and also dictated that desks had to have one side parallel with an adjacent wall. The environment was not exactly conducive to effective working practices, a fact that was tirelessly pointed out by many a jaundiced colleague at the time. However, the promotion changed my grading from seven to ten and from a purely self-interested perspective, things were about to look up.

My new territory seemed positively bespoke by comparison. Now I could wallow in the luxury of a reclining chair offering an almost unlimited range of angular options, at a desk whose relationship to the wall was a matter for the imagination, and on a carpet possessing a pile plush enough to afford me a level of comfort that had not so long before seemed inconceivable. I do recall completely indulging myself for a while in my exciting new workspace, for no better reason than I could.

You may believe this hierarchical approach to the furnishing and fitting of the professional environment to be an exaggeration on my part and that no company would ever function in such a way, but it is all perfectly true. The PMB was formerly a branch of the civil service where such rules were commonplace and, after the Board was formed as an independent body, they were maintained with rigorous zeal by a rather officious personnel manager whose superior manner was irritating enough to keep any self-respecting employee securely locked in his office.

So I now had safely garnered a valuable set of programming skills, acquired a sound, working knowledge of statistics and maximised my use of a good computer on, lest we forget, a particularly decent chair. I was even now the proud owner of a precious copy of Chaseform 1982/83, thanks to my dependable racing ally, Graham (though now I come to think of it, it was meant to be a loan which I must one day return!). Everything pointed towards progress. My search for a winning system had definitely moved up a gear.

Chapter Three

The False Dawn

The 1982/83 jumps formbook featured over 3,000 races and more than 25,000 race performances, so the prospect of transferring it manually to 0the computer was quite daunting. But it was also very exciting. With the data in digital format the options for analysis seemed endless and would surely result in a range of profitable methods, so I believed. The first problem I needed to solve was how to get the contents of the formbook into the microcomputer in a form that could easily be analysed, while at the same time running the statistics department. I considered several different strategies and finally settled for the simplest solution which was borrowed from the elephant eating problem. Question: How do you eat an elephant? Answer: Slice by slice.

My adopted strategy was to reduce the problem to a number of smaller, more easily completed tasks. I decided to take each race type individually, extract the key factors onto paper, type these data items into the computer then use the available software to generate various analyses. As well as FORTRAN and BASIC compilers the old Sirius microcomputers we used had Word Star for letter and report writing, a basic spreadsheet facility, and SPP, a statistics package we used for forecasting and data analysis. They were also fitted with two five-and-a-quarter inch floppy drives but no hard disk which severely limited the maximum file size.

The race grade I chose to analyse first was novices' chases because there were fewer results to enter and they made most appeal from a betting perspective. Due to the size of the data input task it was necessary to keep the number of variables to a minimum so I simply extracted the following factors from each race: month, number of runners in the race, position the favourite ran last time out, position the second favourite ran last time out, finishing position of these two horses in the race under review, their starting prices and the race number. Finishing positions were, for latest run: 1,2,3,4,0,N,-, and for the current race, W, 2, 0. For the last time out data the numbers 1 to 4 represented the finishing positions first to fourth, 0 denoted unplaced but completed, N stood for not complete, and – for no previous run this season. Since I was working from a single formbook I was unable to detect the finishing position for horses having their first run of the season without referring to another book which would have been too time-consuming, hence the need for the seasonal debut indicator.

The indicators W, 2 and 0 for the current race denoted a winner, a placed runner, or an unplaced horse respectively. At home, in the evenings, I would sit with the formbook on my lap and squared paper to my right recoding data for hours. A scanned copy of one of my original data sheets is shown opposite.

I entered these figures into the spreadsheet, added profit

1980/81 NOVICE CHASES (1)

MTH	RNS	LAST TIME 1	LAST TIME 2	THIS TIME 1	THIS TIME 2	PRICE 1	PRICE 2	NO
8	12	–	–	W	P	5/2	7/2	25
	5	–	3	W	O	1	7/4	27
	16	–	–	O	O	9/4	4/1	35
	11	–	–	W	P	7/4	11/4	48
	16	N	2	O	P	2/1	7/2	59
	16	1	N	O	P	4/5	5/2	72
	9	–	2	P	P	9/4	3/1	86
	7	–	N	O	W	11/10	2/1	90
	7	N	–	W	O	4/9	7/1	96
	12	2	–	W	O	2/1	5/2	108
	8	3	2	W	O	8/11	7/2	117
	5	0	1	W	P	7/4	15/8	126
	6	0	1	O	W	15/8	2/1	135
	8	1	3	O	P	8/11	3/1	138
	10	2	–	P	W	5/4	2/1	144
	6	–	0	P	W	7/4	5/2	154
	6	–	–	O	P	11/10	5/2	159
	4	3	–	O	W	8/11	5/2	165
	4	3	0	W	O	8/11	5/4	179
8	14	1	–	P	O	8/11	15/2	190
9	11	N	3	P	W	5/2	3/1	196
	10	1	1	W	P	7/4	15/8	205
	15	1	1	W	P	5/2	4/1	214
	7	–	N	O	W	11/8	10/3	220
	11	1	2	P	O	15/8	3/1	227
	14	0	–	O	P	3/1	5/1	234
	7	2	1	W	O	11/10	9/2	251
	11	N	–	O	P	5/6	6/1	254
	8	–	3	P	O	7/4	2/1	263
	7	1	1	O	O	15/8	5/2	269
	13	1	1	W	O	2/1	3/1	275
	11	1	–	P	W	5/4	3/1	281
	8	N	–	P	W	7/4	3/1	256
	13	N	3	O	O	11/8	7/2	302
	6	1	4	W	P	4/6	10/3	309
	12	2	3	W	P	2/1	9/2	314
	7	–	4	O	P	2/1	11/4	319
	7	3	–	O	P	11/8	3/1	336
	10	N	4	O	O	4/6	11/2	341
	10	2	4	P	O	6/4	7/4	347
	10	–	2	P	P	5/4	4/1	359
	7	3	2	O	P	6/4	7/2	365
9	7	1	2	W	P	7/4	9/4	371
10	9	2	N	W	P	11/8	2/1	378
	14	3	2	W	P	11/8	7/2	383
	11	0	1	O	O	5/2	3/1	391
	14	N	0	O	P	5/2	11/4	404
	14	1	4	P	W	13/8	11/4	408
	3	1	4	W	O	1/2	2/1	413
	12	N	3	W	P	6/4	7/2	418
10	8	0	–	W	P	13/8	3/1	425

Example of manual data recording

and loss figures using a formula, saved the sheet as a data file then analysed it with SPP.

My initial expectations were that favourites which had won their previous race would be the best bets, and those making their seasonal reappearance would be the poorest. From the available racing literature I had gleaned that winning form was supposed to be the best form, and according to the commentators short-priced horses which were untried over fences were poor bets. I had lost count of the times I had heard one of the TV experts say something along the lines of: "The favourite may have the best hurdles form in the race, but he's never jumped a fence in public and won't be carrying any of my money." This seemed sensible and a view with which I agreed until I had analysed the data from the 1982/83 season.

Favourites running after a win had a good win rate but lost almost 5p/£ before tax at starting price. Second favourites were profitable, but the high degree of variability associated with the profit suggested this was down to randomness more than a reliable trend. Horses running after completing but finishing out of the first four were heavy losers, 48p/£, along with market leaders which had failed to complete on their latest start; these lost 50p/£ which was not too unexpected. But the surprising result concerned horses making their seasonal reappearance as favourites: the qualifiers under this rule produced a level stake profit at starting price of 13p/£, and the overwhelming majority of these were horses making their chasing, as well as seasonal, debuts. Clearly the views of the experts were being heeded and their negative comments were making these counter-intuitive selections value bets.

There were a couple of other interesting results as well: favourites which had completed and were running against a second favourite which had failed to get round on its last start were worth noting, as were second favourites running against market leaders which had failed to complete on their most recent run. But basing any system on just one year's data was poor practice so I contacted Raceform and they sold me back editions of the formbook annuals.

It took time extracting the data then entering it at work but I was only caught out once when the finance officer came in during my lunch hour. I quickly looked up from the machine and I'm sure he could tell from the look on my face that I was not doing PMB work, but all he said was, "Sorry, didn't know you were busy I'll catch you later."

With a few years' of data entered the return for the unraced favourites was holding up well, and after a couple of hundred bets was still around the 12p/£ mark. I was convinced I had a workable method.

During the 1987/88 season I put the system into action to £20 stakes, placing bets in the Tote betting office just over the road from the our offices at Broadfield House, in Cowley. The rule was a simple one:

If race type = novices' chase and horse is favourite and horse is making seasonal debut then bet

I also implemented the other two systems to smaller stakes based on the relative finishing positions of the two market leaders on their latest starts: I would back the favourite if it had completed last time out and the second favourite had failed to get round, and vice versa.

However the FTONC (*First Time Out in a Novices' Chase*) method, as I referred to it, was the main system and it provided me with my first implementation problem: how could I tell which horse would start favourite?

This was a basic oversight of the type made by many novice systems players. What I had failed to do was determine how the system was to be implemented before processing the data, or even whether it could be implemented at all.

During the data collection phase, identifying the favourite was a straightforward task since the odds for all runners were listed below each race. But in real time this identification task was not so easily accomplished. Unlike nowadays, bookmakers rarely priced up non-handicap races early in the day with odds normally only available after the first on course show about ten minutes before the off time. There was no way I could keep finding excuses to leave work during the afternoon simply to check the prices at the Tote, so an alternative solution was required.

Obviously I knew which horses could be qualifiers based on their recent performance history, but determining whether they would start favourite or not was down to guesswork. After a few weeks of missed bets, I approached the manager at the shop with a proposal that he found acceptable. I simply wrote on the betting slip "only if absolute favourite", and he agreed to void bets which did not satisfy this stipulation. The secondary systems were still difficult to implement, but I was not too concerned about those.

This relationship worked well and I had the distinct impression that the shop's manager was replicating the bets for himself, maybe with other bookmakers. While I never asked him to confirm my suspicions, he always seemed very happy to pay me out, and on occasion voided some of my bets because the price was too short due to late non-runners for a profit to be made after tax.

By the end of the 1988/89 season the FTONC method had secured a 16p/£ profit, however I had hit another problem. Though the profit was good, the Chancellor was taking more than half of it, since tax on betting stood at ten per cent. I was effectively paying more tax on these bets than some of the highest paid earners in the country paid on their exorbitant salaries, and that was simply not sustainable.

Fortunately I spotted an advert for a bookmakers called Charter House Racing which offered a telephone-based service with only four per cent tax. So, for the 1989/90 season I opened an account and started betting with them. I already had an account with Coral but they had made it clear that "conditional" bets were not acceptable, and they charged the full rate of tax, but Charter House Racing was more than keen to accept bets with provisos and this presented the perfect solution.

The structure of the FTONC method biased selections to the better horses, and as a result many of the runners I backed went on to become top-class performers. I didn't realise it at the time, but that was another angle I could have exploited. During the 1989/90 jumps campaign, qualifiers included Insular, Alone Success, Pantomime Prince, Nohalmdun and Out Of The Gloom, names I am sure will stir plenty of good memories of bets gone by. Watching these horses subsequently, perhaps winning better races at ridiculously short prices, gave me a sense of satisfaction because I had a method that highlighted these runners when they were starting their chasing careers often at much more generous odds. While this did not improve my finances it gave me more confidence in the method I was using, which, for systems followers, is very important.

Each week through the year I received a hand-written statement from Charter House Racing detailing all of my bets and the profit and loss figures, so different from the computer-generated summaries provided by the main firms. Fortunately the FTONC method again performed well turning a profit of just over 15p/£, which equated to 11p/£ after tax.

PROFIT AND LOSS FIGURES FOR THE NOVICES' CHASE FIRST TIME OUT SYSTEM

Year	Profit/£
1981/82	0.303
1982/83	0.130
1983/84	0.005
1984/85	0.102
1985/86	0.034
1986/87	0.229
1987/88	0.192
1988/89	0.164
1989/90	0.153

It was time to review my stake again. I was certain I had found a winning method and was full of confidence for the 1990/91 season. In fact I was so confident I started running computer simulations on the Sirius to see what was going to happen over the next few years if I adopted various progressive staking plans. The results were excellent and my projected retirement date had moved from 2028 to 1995. This was just what I wanted to see, so I decided to start the new season with a stake of £200 per bet, roughly my gross pay for a week, and wait for the money to pour in.

The year 1990 was a pivotal one for me. Sara (the short, dark-haired member of our trip to the Oaks) and I had recently purchased a house based on her modest salary as a teacher and mine from the PMB. However, the ever thoughtful

Chancellor of the Exchequer, Nigel Lawson, decided this was a good time to increase the base rate to 14 per cent, in part to combat rising inflation due to the excessive salaries of workers in the City. At least such stringent action would be an invaluable lesson to future generations not to allow the financial sector, payers of big salaries and even bigger bonuses, to create similar difficulties for the country. And to make matters worse the Halifax Building Society had decided, four weeks after we had purchased the house and moved in, that it would reject one of our two endowment policies because the final projected value "was not guaranteed".

Therefore we had to find an additional £150 per month for a third policy. As it transpired none of the endowment policies purchased at that time were guaranteed, hence the subsequent rebates for all of the mis-sold investments. While the death benefits were fixed, the final accrual rate was variable and there was no way of knowing how much each would finally realise. Clearly the Halifax was also unaware of this lack of a guarantee otherwise it would have rejected all policies rather than a select few.

This financial mishap provides an interesting parallel with betting systems. Endowment policies were sold based on the profit they had made historically. So a salesperson may tell the client that had one been purchased 20 years ago then it would be worth an excessive amount now. We were told that one policy would increase at such a rate that we would be able to pay off the complete mortgage within ten years. In fact the amount accrued by the policy in that time was equivalent to less than ten per cent of the mortgage. It is easy to make the same mistake with betting systems; historical results will never provide a guarantee of future profits.

The reason the endowment policies did not increase in line with expectations was, in part, due to changing circumstances. The recession of the early 1990s resulted in falling share values and house prices which impacted on these investments. The equivalent for betting systems would be changes made by racing's governing body, for instance altering race qualifications, or increasing/decreasing the frequency of certain race types. Though minor, these modifications can have a significant impact on the stability of a betting system which has been derived under a different set of circumstances.

The 1990/91 National Hunt season galloped into action on 3 August and there was a qualifier in the very first novices' chase. Pinemartin started 5/4 favourite for Gordon Richards, and was threatening to destroy the field by the fourth fence. Unfortunately, though, he slipped up after the sixth obstacle. I am certain that the bookmakers had not foreseen such an unlikely outcome but it wasn't going to make them any more charitable. A loss is a loss however bizarre the circumstances.

I had arranged a short West Country camping holiday for Sara and me so that we could get to the races at Newton Abbot and Exeter, and avoid paying the tax. However by the time we reached the course on Haldon Hill on the Wednesday the system was definitely creaking. It had already cost me £600 and I wasn't amused. Following on from Pinemartin's defeat, Sailor's Delight had been well beaten at Market Rasen and Sign Post could only make the runner-up spot at Newton Abbot on the Saturday. This was just the start I was hoping to avoid.

Fortunately it was Sara who came to my rescue. On this one occasion, she took the highly irregular step of withdrawing a large slice of the following month's mortgage money from her account. And so, with a thick wad of notes stuffed reassuringly inside my back pocket and a sharpened sense of duty, I was able to stride through the entrance gates of Exeter racecourse (or Devon and Exeter as it was then known) with the system's reputation teetering on the brink.

The market leaders duly won the first two races and as I shuffled pensively into the betting ring I was banking on the idea that Cut Above Average would make it a hat-trick for the favourites. I took 4/5 to £200 before hastily making my way back to Sara who was by now herself beginning to shift uneasily in the stand. Generally, I don't fear the worst before any race, but that day there was a thick streak of anxiety bisecting us both – even if neither was prepared to admit it to the other. It wasn't the money itself that was on the line here. The stakes were far further north than that. No, I was investing in the very credibility of a freshly born venture that had been three whole years in the making.

The dull pain in the pit of my stomach was a nagging

reminder that this mattered more to me than anything ever had before within the uncertain world of racing. The indigestible reality was dawning that at the end of my once-dazzling racing rainbow was nothing more than a pot of paint, not the serious money-making potential that I'd dreamed of for so long. The number of candlewicks I'd exhausted at both ends had been countless in the relentless, small-hours pursuit of that elusive formula. Although as an avid horseplayer and half-decent mathematician, I could rationalise the reliability of my FTONC system to any sceptic, it simply had to demonstrate its worth and stand on its own two feet. If it failed then so had I.

Like most Martin Pipe-trained horses of that era, Cut Above Average delighted in setting the pace. This time was no different. At the mid-point of the contest, a win seemed the only conceivable outcome. I remember daring just for a brief moment to draw breath as the gap extended promisingly. I should in fact have been enjoying the race at this stage but I simply could not. The tension in my body was tortuous. I was wracked with the kind of nerves I'd never suffered before and, as I contemplated the worst, doubts transformed into fears that haunted and taunted me the larger they loomed. Such a pronounced tremor overtook me at one point that I began to visibly shake. By the time my precious novice approached the last, future-defining fence, a sticky film of sweat had fully lined both forehead and palms. I was desperate to dodge another disappointing defeat.

Cliff Thorburn, the former World Snooker Champion, would often say that pressure was playing a match for $50 with only $20 in your pocket. As Cut Above Average approached the final fence, his definition struck a chord but for slightly different reasons. Although well in front, he was quite evidently on the wrong stride to meet the obstacle with any more than a faint hope of clearing it cleanly. Nevertheless, Cut Above Average negotiated it in less orthodox style, crashing through the fence with jockey Peter Scudamore clinging, limpet-like, to his wavering mount's neck for what seemed like an eternity to his fans in the stands. Would he soon be ditched down on to the carved up ground with all my ambitions spread-eagled hopelessly beside him? Was I staring at the grim prospect of another lost bet and an even worse loss of face?

Somehow, and it's still hard to tell quite how, the champion jockey managed to cling on and clambered back into his saddle on the way to a two-length victory. That day it probably felt as big for me as it was for Pipe. Jubilation all round. The sense of huge relief left us both utterly drained. The system had officially recorded its first winner of the new campaign and it made an overdue and very pleasant change to actually collect. Even so, I knew full well that the system was under-performing and something had to be done to improve it – and fast.

The following day the system found another loser and the pattern seemed to be set. Obviously it is not possible to judge a system on just five bets, but I had a bad feeling that 1990/91 was not going to be a profitable year.

At the end of the season the FTONC system had made a one per cent loss before tax. While this does not appear to be significant, coming after so many years of profit it signalled the end of the method and the realisation that some systems may have a very short life was brought into stark reality. Since then the same selections have averaged a loss of about 10 per cent per year to industry starting price.

The 1990/91 analysis table was covered with minus signs. All three novices' chase systems lost money which included backing the favourite when the second favourite had failed to complete on its latest run, and the reverse system. Quite why this happened is a mystery, perhaps the bookmakers had unearthed the system, maybe other punters had spotted these good betting opportunities and as a result the prices were no longer as generous, or possibly it was merely a statistical anomaly.

Over the next couple of years I tested a few alternative methods, including following the FTONC selections for three further runs which seemed to have potential but soon failed. I noticed that the better runners to back were those which had a hurdles rating of 120 or higher, so I formulated a system based on this and although it was successful there were too few bets to make it worthwhile and in the end I gave up on this particular race type.

In recent years there have been many changes made to the

conditions of novices' chases at the bookmakers' request. The aim is to make them more competitive or, in other words, to make the results more random. This of course helps the layers since it makes the races more closely resemble an equine version of a casino game which is perfect for pricing up and leaves little scope for bettors to make a profit. In addition, the number of novices' chases has been reduced as more maiden chases have been introduced, as well as more novices' handicap chases which are much more difficult to profit from.

However there are a few glimmers of hope for punters keen to devise a system for favourites in novices' chases. Consider the following table which shows the performance of all clear favourites running in novices' or beginners' chases since the 2001/02 season by their most recent finishing position.

ANALYSIS OF ALL NOVICES' AND BEGINNERS' CHASE FAVOURITES BY POSITION LAST TIME

Position LTO	Wins	Runs	Wins%	Profit*/£
Won	580	1166	49.7%	-0.09
2nd or 3rd	633	1334	47.5%	-0.05
Unplaced	399	811	49.2%	0.04
Fell, BD, UR	111	243	45.7%	-0.06
Pulled Up	59	136	43.4%	-0.07
Ref/Ran Out	2	3	66.7%	0.50
All Runners	1784	3693	48.3%	-0.04

* profit given to industry starting price

Interestingly the loss is on the low side at just 4p/£ and, although it may be possible to reduce this further or even turn it into a small profit using the exchanges, there would then be the need to pay the high commission rates which would probably make the approach unusable.

However, there is a group of runners which could form the basis of a profitable system: those which were unplaced on their last start. These 811 runners have made a profit at industry starting price of 4p/£, and those for which exchange prices are available returned a profit of 9p/£ before commission, a very respectable figure. Naturally there are still the same implementation problems concerned with identifying the favourite that I had in the 1980s, but it is a little easier now that bets can be made by computer near to the off time.

ANALYSIS OF ALL NOVICES' AND BEGINNERS' CHASE FAVOURITES THAT WERE UNPLACED LAST TIME BY SEASON

Season	Wins	Runs	Wins%	Profit*/£
2001/02	31	63	49.2%	0.12
2002/03	39	65	60.0%	0.19
2003/04	43	75	57.3%	0.21
2004/05	24	83	28.9%	-0.37
2005/06	33	69	47.8%	0.05
2006/07	41	70	58.6%	0.33
2007/08	37	73	50.7%	0.07
2008/09	33	74	44.6%	-0.01
2009/10	38	78	48.7%	-0.04
2010/11	45	82	54.9%	0.09
2011/12	35	79	44.3%	-0.06

* profit given to industry starting price

There are several advantages to focussing on runners near the front of the market. Firstly, from the bet placement angle there will always be sufficient liquidity on the exchanges to cover the stake, and bookmakers are less likely to close your account after a good run than they are if you are winning off the outsiders. Secondly, with respect to system stability the fact that the prices, and hence the returns from the bets are smaller, means that there is less variation in the sample so a greater degree of confidence about the system's performance can be gained from a smaller number of bets.

It is relatively easy to find long-priced systems that appear to offer great value, especially using exchange prices, but often the summary results mask the fact that the profit is dependent on one or two very big-priced winners, and therefore the reliability of the method is not particularly high. Normally an analysis by price or year will show the degree of variation within the sample and should help to highlight its efficacy.

Taking the qualifiers from the previous table and analysing them by course absence produces the following summary:

ANALYSIS OF ALL NOVICES' AND BEGINNERS' CHASE FAVOURITES THAT WERE UNPLACED LAST TIME BY COURSE ABSENCE

Days Since Last Run	Wins	Runs	Wins%	Profit*/£
1..7	4	9	44.4%	-0.05
8..14	30	68	44.1%	-0.06
15..28	112	214	52.3%	0.13
29..60	90	180	50.0%	0.08
61.100	27	49	55.1%	0.23
100+	136	291	46.7%	-0.0

* profit given to industry starting price

Normally an analysis by course absence will show that runners which are retuning after a short break win at a higher rate and return a lower loss at industry starting price. However, this race grade runs contrary to the usual trend with the most profitable horses found in the 15 to 100 days categories. These horses also produced the highest win rate, exceeding 50 per cent.

One other interesting feature of this pool of horses is that those which have won just a single race from their last three starts made a level stake profit of 19p/£ (298 bets) which is equivalent to 33p/£ at exchange prices.

Systems based on pure data mining, like these, are less reliable than those based on a sound reasoned argument, so whether or not these qualifiers will continue to return a profit is less sure, so extensive testing is required. Methods for determining whether the system has potential to make future profits as well as more general validation techniques are examined later in this text and should always be applied before implementation.

After checking other variations on the FTONC system, the best method I could find required the horse to have started favourite for its last hurdles run and to be rated 120 or higher over hurdles. These runners made a ten per cent profit at industry starting price, but over 14 years there were only 289 qualifiers, and although 115 won, the sample size was far too small to be reliable. However I would now think twice about opposing these runners in future races. The system I am currently using for these races is given in detail in the final chapter along with a selection of other methods.

Chapter Four

Making Contacts

During the 1980s I was a member of a couple of local cribbage teams that played in the Oxfordshire League, as well as a pool team. Crib is still my card game of choice. I never could get interested in poker, though I realise I am now in the minority since it seems to be a game which is gaining popularity day by day, due in no small part to the introduction of online versions and association with celebrity players.

However, 25 years ago the crib league was the place to meet interesting people. While playing a match at the rugby club in Abingdon I met a fellow player who was carrying a leather holdall. We got talking and he told me that he had just come from the local gun club. So we chatted for a while about his sport and I mentioned that, as a fan of Clint Eastwood films, I always wondered what a .44 Magnum handgun was like. "I can help there," he said unzipping his holdall, "Here's one." With that he produced a gun from the bag and passed it to me. At the time we were stood at the bar, in a relatively crowded room, and in my hand I had Dirty Harry's weapon of choice. Obviously I didn't wave it around or point it anywhere in particular, just held it and was shocked by how heavy it was. Nobody paid any particular attention and I assumed the regulars knew about the contents of his bag but it was also rather disconcerting that someone could walk around so casually, as well as consume alcohol, with such a gun in a holdall. Had that happened more recently the club would no doubt have been surrounded by armed response offices within minutes and arrests made.

Although my meeting with the gunman did not convince me to take up target shooting as a sport, playing cards against a chief government scientist did have a significant impact on my future.

Dr David Kelly lived just across the road from the pub where we both played cards. He was a good card player, a genuinely nice person, and extremely intelligent. One evening, while chatting about education over a pint of Morland's bitter, David told me about his postgraduate work and how, as he progressed, the field of study gradually narrowed so that ultimately he was focussing on a very small area of a much larger subject. This intrigued me, because although I wanted to continue in higher education I was keen to target a particular area of computing, specifically artificial intelligence. David went on to tell me that, after completing his first degree, he then studied for a Masters for two years, then completed a PhD, all at different universities. I didn't know it at the time but I was to follow a similar postgraduate path just a few years later.

While the local crib teams included some real characters covering the whole social spectrum, as far as my interest in racing was concerned I made many more helpful contacts through the pool league which tended to include pubs from the Wantage and Lambourn areas. The crib teams were distributed mostly in and around Abingdon.

In November 1986 we played pool against a team at the Greyhound pub in Letcombe Regis. Throughout the evening I thought one of our opponents looked familiar then I realised he was the groom who had led up Western Sunset in the Peterborough Chase at Huntingdon a few days earlier. While I wasn't entirely certain, I decided to ask anyway. Fortunately he was indeed the person I thought and did work for Captain Tim Forster so we chatted about the recent race.

Western Sunset had won this high-quality, small field contest from Half Free and Von Trappe. In fact the first two home met several times throughout their careers and were market rivals at Lingfield when Western Sunset made his second chasing start. Forster's runner was again successful that day which prompted Fred Winter to walk over to the Captain while in the winners' enclosure and tell him that he had a very good horse in his care. Since Fred Winter was such an esteemed horseman and trainer these few words carried a great deal of weight. The lads were already aware of Sunset's ability, though, and had sent a significant bet to the track with one of the grooms who told me recently that he spent the remainder of the afternoon constantly looking over his shoulder. Apparently in those days Lingfield was not the safest place to be carrying a large wad of used notes.

After the pool match I asked Rob (Western Sunset's groom) for his opinion of Co Member who was running later in the week at Wincanton. I had already looked through the form and considered him a very likely winner. Rob assured me that Co Member was in good health but was notoriously lazy at home. However in the context of his usual gallops efforts he had worked well recently with his regular work rider Danny in the saddle. Both lads had been very impressed and were also thinking about backing the horse on his next start. Two days later Co Member won comfortably by seven lengths and though I was not at the track to witness the success, I did manage to get a good bet on. So too did Rob and Danny.

Rob clearly knew his stuff and would become a good friend over the years, along with some of the other lads such as Dave (excellent work rider, marathon runner, top-class rugby player and responsible for Professor Plum, Eastshaw and Coonawarra, among others), Ginge (top-notch work rider who looked after Pegwell Bay and Belgrove Lad) and Danny (another talented work rider who threatened to bare his backside in the market square if Fiddler's Three lost his first chase; unfortunately his usual prescience let him down, costing me a significant sum, but at least the good people of Wantage were saved from the dire spectacle of a half-naked lad from the north east when his double-or-nothing selection was successful).

All the lads used to drink in the Yew Tree pub in Letcombe Bassett just a few yards from Captain Tim Forster's famous stable, which had been home to many Grand National winners including Golden Miller (for a short while), Ben

Nevis, Last Suspect and Well To Do. It was a pub I was to frequent regularly until its closure on New Year's day 1990.

Visits to the stable were also very enjoyable. Normally these took place on Sunday mornings before the pub opened. I remember one day being shown a horse in a box and noticing a very large onion hanging on a string from the rafters near to the animal's head. There must be a good reason for it, I thought, but felt reluctant to ask fearing that my lack of basic knowledge would be cause for amusement among the stable staff. The onion could not have formed any part of the animal's feed, I reasoned, because it was unreachable. Nor, due to its position high in the air, could it have been used as a distraction for an overly curious yet bored horse. There must be a justification I told myself, possibly some form of superstition-based ritual? After much deliberation I still could not determine a logical reason why this horse, Treyford, should be in a box which was adorned in such a fashion. Eventually my curiosity got the better of me and I inquired as to its relevance. "Treyford has breathing difficulties," I was told, "the onion helps take the impurities out of the air." I was amazed at the reply and slightly amused.

Having visited Manton and seen the equine swimming pool, the state-of-the-art boxes and medical resources, I assumed most of the main training establishments had similar facilities. But the modern day advances had clearly bypassed some stables which opted instead for the tried and tested remedies from years gone by. It certainly worked well for Treyford and this relatively lightly-raced chaser won twice from just four starts in the 1987/88 season.

I spent many evenings in the Yew Tree discussing racing with Captain Forster's staff, occasionally also with some of the jockeys. For the most accurate information regarding a runner's fitness and wellbeing I would always take the views of the lads over the jockeys. They seemed to have an instinctive feel for how well the horses they rode, fed and watered were. Naturally no money changed hands. This was merely a group of friends chatting about their work which happened to be horseracing. When we meet up nowadays we often remark that, if they had not all left the sport to pursue alternative careers, horseracing would be off the agenda as a topic for discussion due to the new BHA regulations.

In the wake of the introduction of the betting exchanges, the BHA produced a new set of rules regarding "inside information", essentially information about runners which is not in the public domain. Owners, trainers, and stable employees are no longer allowed to discuss their horses with others if the information passed on is not generally known.

However, it is difficult to see how this can work in practice. For instance, an owner of an unraced juvenile may be told by the trainer that the horse is working exceptionally well and should win his debut. In theory the owner is not allowed to pass this information on to others, whether that is for a financial reward or not. But surely, in such cases, this information will get to close family and friends? And what about his golf partner, or work colleagues? I also cannot believe the pubs in and around Wantage, Newmarket and Lambourn are completely devoid of racing gossip. Even if a stable is completely silent about its runners with not the slightest whisper getting out, the stable employees and owners still have the inside information and are able to use it themselves. Should this also be considered undesirable? If not then the rules are stating that it is acceptable for some bettors to make use of inside information, providing they do not pass it on to others which seems inconsistent at least.

Back in the 1980s there were no such rules and though it was not a system in the purest sense, I did have a method that was proving to be quite profitable. Using the Weekender newspaper I would search for Tim Forster's declared runners, then examine their chances of success using Chaseform Notebook. If I thought a horse had a good chance of winning I would ask the lads for their opinions; if they were positive about the horse's recent work and general health I would back it, price permitting. However if one said that the horse had not eaten up, or had worked sluggishly then I would steer well clear.

One particularly memorable bet concerned a hurdler called Sound Of Islay. Though well bred and related to many good hurdlers, Sound Of Islay had his problems; not physical but mental. I started hearing about this uncontrollable animal in late 1989. Dave was his main work rider but even for a strong experienced jockey, Sound Of Islay was a real handful and not just when he was being put through his paces on the gallops. One frosty morning, on the way to exercise, Sound Of Islay bolted through Letcombe Bassett. The sound of metal hooves skidding violently across the icy tarmac road surface spooked many of the other thoroughbreds and those which remained calm were scattered as the rogue careered through the string. Although this sparsely populated village on the edge of the Ridgeway sees very few cars, a cold dip in the famous watercress beds looked a distinct possibility for both horse and rider. Fortunately crisis was averted when Dave was able to steer him to safety and both escaped uninjured. Just as importantly neither was required to demonstrate their swimming skills.

Working Sound Of Islay was also a major trial. I heard tales of his exploits on a regular basis and it appeared the horse really did not want to go in the direction of the other runners, nor at their slow pace, preferring to take off at full speed whenever the mood took him, in whichever direction he felt like running. However, I also heard that he was useful.

Over time Dave managed to exert a degree of control over this talented wayward animal, and by the late winter he was getting more and more impressed by Sound Of Islay's ability. Then, in early March, I had a phone call in which it was mentioned that "Norm", as he had become affectionately known (named after the Norman Bates character of Psycho fame) had put in an impressive piece of work when easily getting the better of Crystal Bear on the gallops. Dave is not the type of person to exaggerate wildly or to go overboard about a horse, but on this occasion he was very bullish and with good reason. A couple of weeks before Crystal Bear had won a novices' hurdle contest at Stratford by five lengths and I knew he was well thought of by the stable staff. If Sound Of Islay was on a par with him then he was definitely worth a close look in the upcoming novices' race in which he was declared.

Dave did sound a note of caution though. After we had discussed the form of Crystal Bear and the relative merits of Sound Of Islay, he said, "He'll definitely make the frame," paused, and then added, "as long as he stays on the track." Clearly the horse had retained some of his strong spirit, but he also had talent and with this type of runner first time out is normally the best time to back them. Islay's race featured a very short-priced favourite from the Mark Pitman yard which set it up perfectly for an each-way bet.

Unfortunately I was unable to get out of the office near to race time so I had to settle for starting price, and placed my each-way bet with Ladbrokes. When I checked teletext at home I could hardly believe what was written on the screen and had to check with an alternative channel that it was in fact correct and not mis-typed by the operator. Sound Of Islay had beaten Pitman's Do Be Brief (1/3 favourite) by four lengths starting at the incredibly generous price of 33/1. Even now Dave considers this to be one of the highlights of his racing career. Turning a seemingly intractable animal into a winning racehorse is no small achievement. For me it also reinforced the value of this high-quality information and how useful it could be.

Backing long-priced novice hurdlers at industry starting price on their first run is not going to make a long-term profit unless you know something about the horse that others don't. A case could have been made for Sound Of Islay purely on his pedigree since he was a full brother to the top-class Moleboard and a half-brother to Morley Street. But in general these runners lose heavily, over the last few seasons, for instance, approximately 76p/£. These horses are exceptionally poorly priced by bookmakers and, although better prices can be secured on the exchanges, the loss for a similar time period is still remarkably high at 50p/£. Fortunately there are easier ways to profit from this particular race type and these are outlined later.

This information exchange worked well for many seasons, but I needed equivalent contacts in flat racing stables for the summer. Through the pool matches I did manage to make a couple of contacts in Henry Candy's stable, and this resulted in some nice wins including Ben Adhem in the City & Suburban Handicap at Epsom but there were many failed gambles.

A notable example concerned an unraced two-year-old named Navajo. Apparently he was a real speedster so we went to Windsor on a warm Monday evening in June 1988 to back him. In the paddock he was not the obvious favourite for the race, so it was surprising that he opened as short as he did, around the 5/4 mark. I discussed his appearance with one of the stable staff and was assured he was a compact type who had plenty of speed; the ideal sprinter. So I backed him at 11/8 and then watched the race from the stands with Sara, the stable contact and a few others. It was soon clear that our money was lost and Navajo was well beaten into seventh. At the finishing line the only person smiling was Sara who had used her own system to back the winner, Tread Lika Prince, on the Tote at £27.20. Sara's system, which she still maintains is better than any of mine, is very simple: back the runner whose jockey is wearing the same colours as West Ham football players (the home strip naturally).

Though placed on occasions, Navajo did not make the winners' enclosure that year and it was clear that the "Candy" information was not as helpful as that I received from the Forster boys. Fortunately I had a route to information in a different flat racing stable via another contact. His name was Miles.

Chapter Five

Million-Dollar Two-Year-Olds

Miles was a close friend of Graham, who had lent me the formbook around the time I was busy developing the novices' chase system. A lean, towering figure with just enough beard to lend his angular features an air of mystery, Miles was a bricklayer by trade and somewhere to the left of Karl Marx where his political leanings were concerned. In those days, he was also a heavy bettor and an even heavier drinker. This last detail first came to my notice during one particular house party at which Miles and I first became acquainted. As memory serves, we chatted earnestly, and at some considerable length about our shared passion for racing.

Imagine my surprise therefore, when only a matter of a few days later beside the main parade ring at Newbury, he seemed hardly to recognise me. Over time, as we continued to strike up a strong racing rapport in a whole host of licensed premises, it became increasingly apparent that it must have been the drink (or the actual quantity of it to be exact) that had blighted his memory of me that day. Once he had been reminded of our initial meeting, we spent the afternoon vigorously scrutinising the form and chasing winners and by the last race we had formed the foundation of a firm friendship.

Sara and I would meet Miles and Gill (his wife) and two of

their best friends Jean and Tom, at a variety of hostelries which took in places as far flung as Kingston Lisle, Letcombe Bassett and Bishopstone. We often found ourselves amid stunning landscapes and, as Sara settled into the chauffeuring role, I found myself able to ponder future plans while delighting in some of middle England's most breathtaking views, especially when our route followed the Downs road as it clings to the foot of White Horse Hill. Buried deep in racing country the ancient monument's presence always conjured up thoughts of races gone by as well as races to come, so it always seemed fitting that this particular stretch near Uffington was so often part of our journey home.

The company was always entertaining and the talk lively. Gill was a budding archaeologist who related tales of wandering around Wiltshire fields, straining to discover another ancient gem. Jean, a Friends of the Earth activist, kept us up to speed on the latest green issues, while Tom's literary background gave rise to some very informative discussions. All in all, albeit a little the worse for wear on occasions, I would generally coast back home feeling very satisfied by another very convivial evening.

Other friends, including Graham and Alan, would also join us from time to time, and although the make-up of the group fluctuated a little, the constant thread linking the conversation was unswervingly racing. Not that Jean and Tom were naturally that way inclined but Miles was utterly absorbed in the sport and I could not help but be hugely impressed by his insight and depth of knowledge.

Miles had what I like to term reliable contacts in the Jeremy Tree stable and had avidly studied the yard's runners for some years. By this point, he could tell me what Tree was about to do with a horse before the great trainer could have done himself. Many punters I've encountered have had preferred stables and followed their runners religiously, sometimes utilising jockey and trainer combination systems in the process. However, in Miles's eyes such favouritism was as untrustworthy as it was unqualified. Even so, where the Beckhampton yard was concerned, having his inside track would pay sizeable dividends on more than one occasion on the outside track itself!

Jeremy Tree was a canny, systematic operator and his runners followed paths as well chosen as the tracks they'd navigate on the courses themselves. For example, his best two-year-old filly would always make her debut at Newbury, and normally in one particular maiden contest by the name of the West Ilsley Stakes. How he would fare today, in an era bedevilled by so much BHA tinkering, is uncertain but in the more stable, predictable decade that was the 1980s, his training methods were seriously effective.

Gill and Miles were older than Sara and me, and had partied through the sixties and seventies, so the eighties were not going to be any different and it wasn't long before we were invited to their home for an informal gathering where it seemed the alcohol flowed faster than the river Thames.

Many of Tree's stable staff supplemented the regular pub-visiting crowd and it was a lively occasion full of wit much drier than Miles's plentiful bar. A particular highlight worthy of mention was my receipt of a memorable invitation. It would lead to an experience which was to leave a lasting mark on my ambitions for many years afterwards. I was asked if I would be interested in taking a tour of the Beckhampton stables the following morning. Never having been naturally inclined to harmonise personally with the dawn chorus, the prospect of an early start still didn't faze me until I learned that I would be expected no later than five o'clock.

Refreshed by at the very most a two-hour nap, I found myself being whisked through the early morning mist to Tree's yard where we were to collect the groom who had offered the invitation. Once Neil was on board, we journeyed a number of miles further into the remote heartlands of Wiltshire, a county (so history reveals) that was at one time home to more pigs than people. The explosion of the Swindon conurbation required to house part of the country's exponentially increasing population, later put paid to that particular anomaly but meandering through this remote region at this unearthly hour was indeed an eerie exercise.

Flanking our route were vast fields of wheat which seemed to stare back at us in their serried ranks. These guardians of the countryside were apparently questioning how we might dare disturb their solitude. Or perhaps that feeling was just the previous evening's intake charging my imagination and reminding me of the last time I'd felt so alive in the middle of the night. It was at a midsummer solstice I had once spent observing a Druid ceremony within a circle of stone not far from this spot.

Eventually we came to an abrupt halt just outside a barn of quite imposing dimensions. Neil slipped a key into what seemed like an unfittingly feeble padlock and heaved the main door open. I was immediately captivated by the absolute splendour of the sight that greeted us. The building was awash with racehorses in their perfect prime – muscles all finely honed and luxurious coats you could part your hair in. I tiptoed respectfully between the two rows of boxes. Neil dutifully supplied names, pedigree and form while we looked on agog. For me, a vivid recollection remains of the occupant of one stall (it was the second one on the left) inside which stood an especially imperious filly. At the time, I knew as much about this horse as Jeremy Tree plainly did about security, given the ease with which anyone could have gained access to that barn, but Neil didn't delay in providing the crucial factfile and could barely contain his excitement in so doing.

With a kind of rustic purr he exclaimed, "This is Magic Of Life, she's an unraced two-year-old and cost over $2.5m." He paused before adding, almost matter-of-factly, "She's the best two-year-old filly in the country." Miles was beaming contentedly. He was already fully familiar with the promise of his latest equine phenomenon and was probably savouring my stunned reaction as the enormity of Neil's casual assertion began to penetrate.

At Newbury, a week or so later, we waited in the Silver Ring, where we believed we could achieve the best early price, rather than in the main betting area as usual. Searing guitar was still reverberating in my head. It was always the same. If I felt truly confident before a day's racing I would opt for the full-volume accompaniment throughout the 30-mile journey to the track. Only the very best of the blues you understand. Usually it was Clapton, but often Cray or King (BB) who would complement the upbeat mood perfectly. On days such as these, I can remember that irrepressible sense of something beyond optimism – something closer to destiny.

There were several of us who had gathered including Miles and a few other members of the Beckhampton team. On this day, though fused with a fair degree of tension, the pre-race banter crackled and fizzed along. Spirits were soaring. We had come to back the best juvenile filly in the country. The plan was to take the first price once it became available to a couple of layers. It was an agonisingly anxious wait. I became hopelessly preoccupied with a wristwatch whose hands appeared to have stopped dead for what seemed like an eternity.

Eventually, one brave bookmaker chalked up his odds (9/4). A couple more swiftly followed and we were in. The money was on. Back in the main ring Magic Of Life was trading at 15/8, and by off-time was down to 11/8. We had beaten the book, and it was now up to Magic Of Life to beat the ten opponents which included the well-fancied Jodoka from the powerful Barry Hills yard.

Perhaps surprisingly, I remember feeling completely at ease before that race, even though my stake was all together more substantial than I was used to risking in those days. In this regard, a clear pattern has emerged over a long period. Whenever I back a runner on someone else's advice, the pressure's off as far as I'm concerned. While I may have a greater financial stake in the outcome of the contest, I never have the same emotional investment as I do when a tip is derived from one of my systems and it's someone else's money on the line.

When the field pounded past the furlong marker the pulse did start to quicken apace, as our superstar-in-the-making began to prove her class and surged clear of the competition. By the time the winning line was looming, she had left a decent set of horses trailing in her wake. Magic Of Life was the quite glorious victor and it felt good.

So, was Magic Of Life the best juvenile filly in the country? Well, on that famous day at Newbury she may have been, but later in the season she was soundly beaten by Henry Cecil's future Classic winner Diminuendo who looked a very special two-year-old in that company. Even so, it was Magic Of Life who ended her first year with victory in the Mill Reef Stakes, when putting paid to a trio of notable challengers in the form of Intimidate, Rahy and Ship Of Fools.

On her reappearance as a three-year-old she herself was put to the sword in the 1,000 Guineas by Ravinella, before turning the tables in an avenging triumph over the same opponent in the Group 1 Coronation Stakes at Royal Ascot. So, though the truly magical circumstances of our very personal introduction still flicker warmly in the memory, Magic Of Life, though undoubtedly good, was probably not quite as good as her inflated price tag had had me first believe.

It was not long after we had happily collected at Newbury that I first turned my thoughts to creating a system based on two-year-old favourites and their first start. Back at home, I committed myself totally to the Flat formbooks I owned, meticulously extracting the data in a similar way I did for the novices' chases. Though I spent many painstaking hours organising and analysing the data, the viable, readily applicable approach I hoped to find remained elusive. This was probably due to the variables I chose to use and emphasised how important this phase of system development is in unlocking the overall system-creation process.

Magic Of Life, it occurred to me, was made favourite for many reasons: clearly some people knew she was well above average; she was trained by one of the best trainers in England; and she was first raced at his local track in a race he had consistently used to catapult the careers of many a good horse of times past. Then there was the small matter of her price – all $2.5 million of it. All these factors contributed to her market value, but starting at 11/8 she was still overpriced and this was due to two key factors. Firstly, Newbury was a top-class racecourse that attracted good juveniles from the main stables, thus producing a higher-than-average degree of competition. Secondly, she had never raced before. So therein lay the basis of a worthwhile system but I needed to gain access to a range of data I could not easily extract from the formbook, where the variables I had been able to analyse were not sufficiently significant to return a reasonable profit.

However, with access to a computer database of historical results, it is now possible to investigate these horses more closely. The first table presents the win rate statistics for all juveniles running in non-handicap races; this gives an overview of how these horses perform relative to their starting prices.

ANALYSIS OF ALL JUVENILE NON-HANDICAP RACES BY STARTING PRICE

Starting Price	Wins	Runs	Wins%	Profit*/£
Odds On	493	854	57.7%	-0.07
Ev-2/1	718	1973	36.4%	-0.07
9/4-4/1	960	4343	22.1%	-0.10
9/2-6/1	442	3158	14.0%	-0.14
13/2-10/1	498	5179	9.6%	-0.13
11/1-16/1	281	5385	5.2%	-0.25
18/1-33/1	196	6999	2.8%	-0.29
40/1+	53	7984	0.7%	-0.64
All Runners	3641	35875	10.1%	-0.29

* profit given to industry starting price

The 35,875 runners returned an average loss to a level £1 stake of 29p, which shows the size of the problem facing starting price bettors in this race type. There is a reasonable bias to the front of the market though, with juveniles priced at 2/1 or lower losing just 7p/£ and this does suggest that it is the shorter-priced horses we should be focussing on.

An analysis by run number shows only a minimal difference between the categories which implies that the debut runners are not under-priced anymore than the more experienced horses.

ANALYSIS OF ALL JUVENILE NON-HANDICAP RACES BY RUN NUMBER

Run No.	Wins	Runs	Wins%	Profit*/£
1st Run	888	12594	7.1%	-0.28
2nd Run	1214	9812	12.4%	-0.28
3rd Run	761	6960	10.9%	-0.27
4th Run	329	2738	12.0%	-0.36
5th Run	201	1614	12.5%	-0.29
6th+ Run	248	2157	11.5%	-0.24
All Runners	3641	35875	10.1%	-0.29

* profit given to industry starting price

However, while the win rate is remarkably consistent for horses that have previously raced, it is markedly lower for debut runners at just over seven per cent. Any system which reflected this low win rate would be difficult to follow due to the very long losing runs.

The aim was to generate a system based on well-regarded debutante juveniles. This should help to increase the success rate since these runners are likely to be drawn from the front of the market and that will make the system easier to run. The following table breaks down the debut runners by starting price.

ANALYSIS OF ALL FIRST RUN JUVENILES IN NON-HANDICAP RACES BY STARTING PRICE

Starting Price	Wins	Runs	Wins%	Profit*/£
Odds On	26	46	56.5%	-0.04
Ev-2/1	102	267	38.2%	-0.01
9/4-4/1	205	977	21.0%	-0.12
9/2-6/1	154	980	15.7%	-0.02
13/2-10/1	165	1868	8.8%	-0.19
11/1-16/1	125	2322	5.4%	-0.23
18/1-33/1	83	3157	2.6%	-0.32
40/1+	28	2977	0.9%	-0.51
All Runners	888	12594	7.1%	-0.28

* profit given to industry starting price

An even stronger bias to the short-priced juveniles is apparent and the much lower average loss per bet is a promising result suggesting that bettors are shying away from these unraced runners to a certain degree.

Isolating juveniles that started as absolute favourites on their first run returns a 14p/£ loss, much higher than those priced at up to 2/1. However keeping to the grade A courses, namely Ascot, Goodwood, Newbury, Newmarket, Sandown and York, produces the following results:

UNRACED JUVENILE FAVOURITES AT GRADE A TRACKS	
Colts and geldings:	+1p/£ from 119 runners
Fillies:	-27p/£ from 51 runners

The return for fillies is exceptionally poor, however the colts and geldings made a slight profit at starting price which at exchange prices increased to 14p/£. Clearly the exchange layers are underestimating the chance of success of these horses more so than the traditional bookmakers.

If these horses are known to be above average then it is reasonable to expect them to shorten during the day. Therefore it may be beneficial to back the qualifiers at morning prices rather than close to off time, though this does require the bettor to predict whether or not a horse will start favourite. But with just 119 qualifiers this method is not worth a great deal of effort to implement, furthermore its future is far from certain based on such a small sample size. An alternative to this is to monitor the price of the horse during the day and then back it on the exchanges at off time if it meets certain criteria.

An examination of exchange price moves shows that over the last five years backing all debut-run juveniles at the price available at the official off time for the race that had reduced in price, compared to that available at 10.30am, returned a level stake profit of 23p/£ for those starting at 5.0 or lower. Essentially this method isolates those juveniles on their first racecourse run which are well fancied and have been supported during the day. In order to make the price comparison it is necessary to normalise both sets of prices to a 100 per cent book which removes the effect of horses withdrawn after the first price was recorded.

Monitoring prices during the day is not easy for many bettors, so a trainer-based method rather than a priced based method can be employed. One approach would be to analyse the debut-run juveniles by trainer, and then select the stables which have shown a good profit in the recent past with a view to following them through the year. For the 2012 turf season this list would probably have included: Ann Duffield, John Gosden, Charles Hills, Sir Henry Cecil, Mark Johnston, Mahmood Al Zarooni, Richard Fahey, Richard Hannon, Ralph Beckett, and Saeed Bin Suroor, all of whom have excellent records with juveniles making their debuts.

Using a fixed list of trainers provides an easy-to-run system that may return a profit. However, if you have access to a database of results, such as that provided by Raceform Interactive, it is possible to make the trainers to follow list more dynamic and more responsive to the patterns of current results. For example the list can be updated on a day-by-day basis by including the latest available data. So, if a trainer is experiencing a poor year, it will form part of the analysis and could mean that the trainer was dropped from the list, while others may be added through the season. In order to implement such an approach it is necessary to use a strict rule for qualification either based on profit or win rate.

My preference, for this particular method, is for win rate. The analyses produced earlier showed that the average success rate for all debut juveniles is seven per cent, so my rule would be:

> The trainer qualifies if the first run win rate > 7%

The previous analysis tables also suggested that we should be focussing on the front of the market and excluding fillies, so the betting rule could become:

> Back all debut-run juvenile colts and geldings on turf if the trainer's win rate for all debut runners is greater than 7% and the exchange price near to the off time is at most 5.0.

Using this rule over the latest four seasons available produced 385 bets and a level stake profit before commission of 14p/£. In total there were 134 winners which equates to a success rate of 34 per cent which should ensure that losing runs are not too long, but even that good win rate did produce a losing run of 11 during the period.

While the trainer approaches have some merit they are susceptible to the adverse effects of changing external factors. For instance a trainer may lose a key owner whose horses have contributed significantly to the stable's previous good performance; or the yard may be hit by a virus that would adversely affect the performance of the runners. However by checking for such scenarios and modifying the betting strategy accordingly, it is possible to use these methods to good effect.

Though I could not make a worthwhile system for juvenile favourites on their first run in 1987, a race the following season gave me an idea that did prove to be profitable. Jeremy Tree had had a good summer winning the West Ilsley Stakes as usual, this time letting Willie Carson steer Stellaria to an easy four-length success, as well as having future star in Danehill in his care. But it was Major Dick Hern who had the strongest hand with respect to juveniles.

Our main summer break was organised, as usual, around the racing calendar. The plan, as per the previous year, was to attend Newbury's two-day August meeting then drive up to York so that I could treat Sara to the three-day Ebor festival, under canvas again, of course.

I met Miles by Newbury's pre-parade ring on the Friday. His full beard had given way to a better shaped "Van Dyke" and his heavily suntanned skin, contrasting markedly with his prematurely greying hair, was evidence of long hours spent in the sun on the various building sites of Wiltshire that summer. The dull orange tie he was sporting was not in keeping with the rest of his attire, which featured a light-grey jacket over a blue shirt, and I immediately guessed why.

"Forgot your tie again?" I asked with a grin. Miles shrugged and cast his eyes skywards in silent confirmation, and I wondered just how much money Newbury made from renting out ties to the absent-minded among us.

"Are you backing Hern's best two-year-old?" he asked, while noting the runners as they paraded around the oval ring in front of us.

"Of course," I replied, believing he was referring to Prince Of Dance who was scheduled to run in the Washington Singer Stakes that afternoon. The Sadler's Wells colt had won his debut run in good style and looked like a potentially useful juvenile.

"So you'll be here tomorrow then?" he added with a grin.

"Yes I will, but I'm not sure what you mean."

"I'll explain later," he added and turned back to the horses.

I was slightly put out. Miles was not usually this guarded, but I didn't pursue it and we moved to the main stand to watch the first race, a big field apprentices' handicap that made no appeal from a betting angle.

Later in the afternoon Prince Of Dance strolled away with the Listed race with Carson merely pushing the colt out for a six-length victory. Unfortunately, for his connections, he was later to be disqualified because he was not qualified for the race due to his sire's winning record. However he really did look like a very good colt and in my mind the best two-year-old of the year. Miles was also impressed by the manner of the win, but I knew he was holding something back.

"I wonder how good Dick Hern's best two-year-old is then?" he said.

"That is his best two-year-old," I replied, "probably the best in the country."

"Okay, I'll own up. I've a new contact at Hern's and his best two-year-old runs tomorrow. He's called Nashwan."

I did not believe Miles at first, but he was adamant, according to his contact, Nashwan was a much better horse than Prince Of Dance, and victory on Saturday was, apparently, a formality.

Arriving at the course the following day, earlier than usual, I pushed through the turnstiles and had the same calming feeling I always had at the start of a racing day. It was like entering a racing bubble. Events in the outside world were completely irrelevant; aliens could land in Piccadilly Circus and I would be totally unaware until I left the track. The only thing on my mind was horses.

This day I was also feeling supremely confident. In my possession I had information that, according to my betting colleagues, would mean I would end the day with much more money than I started it with. Miles arrived late, missing the first race completely. And unusually for him he didn't bet in the next three contests; he was betting in just one race and on just one horse.

I'm not sure how much he eventually got on Nashwan, but in the final minutes before the off he was running round the ring taking prices and passing on his information to friends and other punters. I managed to get 9/4 on the rails using one of my credit accounts, and settled for just one bet. For some reason my confidence was fading as the race time approached. Maybe it was the field size, I always found big fields off-putting, and there were 27 at the post. Also the Hern stable contact was new. Could his judgement be trusted?

We took up our usual positions in the members' stand, almost in line with the finishing post and waited for the race to start. Given Miles's strong political views, I found it slightly contradictory that we always paid extra to watch the races from the most expensive of Newbury's three enclosures. It was not as if we had significantly better viewing than we had from the main ring, also a dress code was imposed, hence the need for a tie, but at least hats were not compulsory as they are for the Royal meeting at Ascot. Miles was a "man of the people", a fully paid-up member of the "workers party", an advocate of egalitarianism and an anti-capitalist at heart, yet we stood in the premium enclosure with barriers, gates, and racecourse staff employed to separate those who chose to pay more from the other racing enthusiasts. I appreciate that his political hero, Karl Marx, felt that, along with religion gambling was the opiate of the masses, but the close association Miles had with one of the most elitist sports must have caused him a degree of conflict.

The race itself proved the Hern contact to be correct; Nashwan won a shade comfortably then on his next start took an Ascot Listed race. As a three-year-old he won the

2,000 Guineas as well as the Derby and was clearly one of the best middle-distance horses of the decade. The information was sound, and we all made a nice profit, and while we were celebrating our win Miles pressed £500 in £50s into my hand. "That's for Danehill at York, okay?" he said, "Get the best price you can." Of course I didn't mind, I would be at the track and able to place the bet without any problem, and also without any tax, I just had to remember to take it with me. It was interesting that Miles did not give me any price stipulations which I am sure many value punters would find difficult to accept.

Danehill won the Convivial Stakes in comfortable fashion and Miles was pleased with his £400 profit but what we didn't know then was the profound effect this horse would have on thoroughbred breeding for the next 15 years. As a three-year-old he ran third to Nashwan in the Guineas but was later switched to shorter distances and ended the season as Champion Sprinter. His career as a sire is legendary and I doubt there is a punter anywhere in the world who has not put a few pounds on one of his progeny. That's one of the most appealing aspects of the sport. A horse carrying your money that is just a name and set of colours in the newspaper today, may one day be responsible for champions the world over and though he may be owned by Khalid Abdullah or Godolphin, for those few seconds of the race he's your horse.

It had been a great day at Newbury, but on the way home the same thoughts crossed my mind that did after Magic

Of Life's win the previous year. How could these horses be exploited with a systematic approach?

Over the next few weeks I started analysing these races in detail, and eventually I realised that my search had to move from one of finding a systematic way of identifying the potentially profitable top-class debut runners, to using their characteristics to highlight good future bets. So rather than adopting an "on the day" system, I needed to move to a "horses to follow" approach. This idea was spawned by the fact that a high proportion of non-juvenile Group 1 winners started favourite for their first run as two-year-olds, and an even higher proportion made the frame on this run. These attributes, along with the identification of the course where they made their debuts, could be used to identify potentially smart runners which were worth following.

The final version of the system essentially concerned noting juveniles that were beaten as favourites for their debut run at certain tracks then following them for at most three starts, stopping if they won.

Over the next few seasons and well into the mid-1990s this method worked exceptionally well. In fact I included it and two other variations in my first book: *Flat Racing For Profit* published by Raceform in 1996 and now available as a free download from my website. At that stage the previous five year profit for the method was a staggering 53p/£ at industry starting price. However, from then onwards the returns started to drop and the final death knell for the system was sounded by the BHA when they made dramatic changes to the two-year-old race programme a few years ago.

The performance of this method over time highlights perfectly how changing environmental factors can turn a winning method into a losing one. Since the turn of the century the number of juvenile races run on turf has been reduced from a figure of over 900 per year, to one as low as 808 in 2006, while the number of races in total has increased significantly. But more importantly the number of conditions stakes races has dropped from 145 in 2002 to just over 80 in 2011. These races are viewed as less competitive and therefore less profitable to bookmakers, hence the reduction. Such a change would not, at first sight, appear to have any relevance to the system I used, but in fact the seemingly innocuous modifications to the programme, significantly changed the way trainers placed their two-year-old runners and consequently affected any system based on juveniles to follow.

The scrapping of many of the stakes events means that an above-average horse, winning its maiden on its debut run, now has fewer options for its second start. Obviously if it is thought to be top class then it can make the step up to a pattern race, otherwise it has to take the handicap route from mid-July onwards. Historically the conditions stakes races provided a stepping stone for good horses between maiden races and pattern company and could be used to gain further experience. Without them the trainer is faced, in the early season, with a difficult decision of whether to start the career of a potentially useful horse or not, and it appears that many are opting not to, and are waiting until very late in the season before taking their better runners to the track.

So as well as disrupting the "juveniles to follow" method, another effect of these changes is the downgrading of the early season pattern events especially the Royal Ascot juvenile races. Run in June, these races are now far too early in the season, and though they once were key contests in the calendar attracting top-class runners, these events are now no better than average, and would equate to modest Listed events in the 1990s.

Betting systems thrive on stable conditions, so changes such as these are never welcome. However after a period of time new patterns become established and can be exploited by the system player. While the original "juveniles to follow" system is unlikely to return a profit in the future, it is worth noting that, at the time of writing, backing all two-year-olds that were beaten on their debut run at Ascot, Goodwood, Haydock, Newbury, Newmarket or Salisbury on their next start, providing they are priced at no longer than 4/1, has made a profit of 14p/£ on the exchanges from the last 1252 bets. No doubt this pattern will change over the next few years but it is worth monitoring and the idea underlying it is worth remembering for future systems.

One of the features that makes two-year-old racing so interesting is that the horses are growing physically and, as a result, are improving, in some cases dramatically. This gradual improvement throughout the season adds another aspect to assessing them in terms of form or speed ratings. For the older horses this is not such a problem because once they have raced several times, the chance of further improvement will be diminished and normally will only occur due to a change in circumstances, as the result of a medical intervention, or more commonly, due to a change in racing conditions. For juveniles, improvement is a natural process and consequently it should form part of the ratings procedure.

Most two-year-olds make the greatest amount of improvement from their first to second run which is due to experience and in some cases fitness. Analysing the change in performance ratings for the first two runs for juveniles can provide valuable information for assessing the likely degree of improvement for other runners since these figures are closely linked to trainer and sire. Runners from some stables improve significantly on their second start compared to their debut run and similar patterns can be found with respect to sires.

The effect of this change is reflected in the win rate for these horses. Juveniles tend to win at a rate of about 7 per cent on their first racecourse appearance; this figure increases to 12.5 per cent for their next start (see earlier table). However the profit and loss figures demonstrate that this is already fully accounted for by the layers since for both runs the average loss is 28p/£ at industry starting price. For horses near the front of the market the second run loss is not as great (-8p/£) but it is still significant.

While the first to second run improvement seems to be well known, it is not clear that the degree of improvement associated with the physical development of the horse is fully accounted for in the price. For instance, if a juvenile is off the course for a couple of months this is normally viewed as a negative by bettors and bookmakers, which in some cases would be correct. But how many would also consider the fact that during these two months there is a good chance that the horse has improved physically and hence should be rated higher than when last seen on a racecourse? The data suggests not all do so.

The following table shows the performance of all juveniles priced at up to 10/1 (starting price) running in non-handicap races in Great Britain over a five-year period by days off the track.

ANALYSIS OF ALL JUVENILE NON-HANDICAP RACES BY DAYS SINCE LAST RUN FOR HORSES PRICED UP TO 10/1 (STARTING PRICE)

Course Absence (days)	Wins	Runs	Wins%	Profit*/£
1..7	134	563	23.8%	-0.03
8..14	687	3118	22.0%	-0.12
15..28	1110	5023	22.1%	-0.10
29..60	430	2178	19.7%	-0.16
61..100	86	398	21.6%	0.08
101+	12	89	13.5%	-0.51
Unraced	652	4138	15.8%	-0.12
All Runners	3111	15507	20.0%	-0.11

* profit given to industry starting price

The 61 to 100 days group is of interest since it covers horses off the track for roughly eight to 14 weeks. These 398 runners have won at a rate of a little better than one in five, and have returned a profit of 8p/£ which translates to 26p/£ at exchange prices. But why is the return for horses off the track for over 100 days so poor by comparison? The reason could be that these horses have been off the track for so long due to a physical ailment, whereas those in the 61-100 day category may have been waiting for suitable conditions, or given time to progress from one run to the next, or simply due to a lack of suitable races. This is supported to a degree by the following table which shows that these qualifiers running after a win make an even better profit at starting price.

ANALYSIS OF ALL JUVENILE NON-HANDICAP RACES BY POSITION ON LAST RUN FOR HORSES PRICED UP TO 10/1 (SP) AND OFF THE TRACK FOR 61 TO 100 DAYS

Position Last Time	Wins	Runs	Wins%	Profit*/£
Won	15	68	22.1%	0.16
2nd or 3rd	23	96	24.0%	0.03
Unplaced	48	232	20.7%	0.09
All Runners	86	396	21.7%	0.09

* profit given to industry starting price

The final issue that needs addressing is whether horses returning to the track for their second run after a break of between 61 and 100 days do better than would be expected.

From the following table it can be seen that they do with

a strike rate of better than one in four and a level stake profit to industry starting price of 24p/£ (43p/£ at exchange prices). Furthermore, horses on their third run are also worth noting, having made a profit of 23p/£ which on the exchanges was in fact over 50p/£.

ANALYSIS OF ALL JUVENILE NON-HANDICAP RACES BY RUN NUMBER FOR HORSES PRICED UP TO 10/1 (SP) AND OFF THE TRACK FOR 61 TO 100 DAYS

Run Number	Wins	Runs	Wins%	Profit*/£
First Run	0	0	0.0%	0.00
Second Run	43	169	25.4%	0.24
Third Run	33	133	24.8%	0.23
Fourth Run	9	65	13.8%	-0.16
Fifth Run	1	17	5.9%	-0.83
Sixth Run	0	14	0.0%	-1.00
All Runners	86	398	21.6%	0.08

* profit given to industry starting price

Juvenile races are, without doubt, the most interesting Flat racing contests. From the pure sporting angle these races can feature relatively unknown horses which may one day become champions, and unlike handicaps where the runners are fully exposed and likely to finish in a bunch, it is quite possible that a juvenile race produces a winner that is simply a class above his or her opposition and takes the event in a style that cannot fail to impress any of the spectators. Arazi's win in the USA was one of the most spectacular races I have ever witnessed, and more recently the runs by Johannesburg, as well as the ten-length success by Galileo on his only two-year-old start, are races that stay in the memory for a very long time.

For race analysts these contests provide good opportunities for making a profit. The fact that they are more difficult to price accurately, due to the many unknowns, separates them from other races and creates an environment where a knowledgeable bettor can employ many relatively unconsidered factors to his or her advantage.

Chapter Six

Challenging Races: Three-Year-Old Handicaps

Neither Miles nor I had a great deal of time for handicap races. The exceptions for Miles were three-year-old only handicaps, and those contests which featured a runner from Beckhampton. It was natural for Miles to have an interest in races in which a horse from the Jeremy Tree stable was declared, but for him to bet in the other three-year-old handicaps was difficult to understand. However Miles had a theory about this particular race classification, a system really, though he would not have admitted it. His approach was simply to find an improving horse. I tended to agree with Peter Braddock's sentiments expressed in his excellent book *Braddock's Guide to Horse Race Selection and Betting* that handicap races represent a poor medium for making a profit.

Fortunately there were far fewer handicaps then than now, when the primary aim of the sport was to determine the ability hierarchy of the horse population under various racing conditions and encourage people to bet. Nowadays the emphasis has been placed on maximising bookmakers' profits and, as a result, racing's income. When tax (including the levy contribution) was required to be paid on each bet it was in the interest of the sport to have as many bets placed as possible. Therefore certain types of race, in which finding winners was more straightforward, made up a larger proportion of events. A punter who backs a winner is more likely to have another bet than one who loses, and more bets meant more money for racing.

The focus has now shifted and racing's revenue is based on bookmakers' profits so the aim is to relieve punters of their cash as quickly as possible, thus increasing profits. This has lead to significant changes to the race programme, including a rapid increase in the number of handicaps. Naturally the bookmakers claim that bettors prefer handicaps and competitive racing, and while there's no doubt that some do, I am not sure this is the real reason for the changes. Now that the layers have such control over horseracing the sport's ever-increasing reliance on handicaps is a trend that is unlikely to be reversed.

Given our general ambivalence to handicaps I was surprised to receive an early morning telephone call (8-30am was early for me at the weekend) from Miles on the Saturday of Newbury's August meeting in 1987 in which he simply gave me the name of a handicapper. In fact all he said was, "Timefighter's off today. Get on early." The strict interpretation of his comment was that Timefighter had not been trying in his previous races but would be running on his merits today. This wasn't the case at all. Timefighter was a useful, improving three-year-old who had won a handicap earlier in the season before running well below par in Listed and stakes races. These poor efforts would improve his price, and if he had been working well at home then there was little doubt that he was a value bet. I took the 8/1 at 9.30am with the intention of topping up at the track.

At Newbury, Miles's beard practically bristled and his ever-amiable grin broadened just a little wider, such was the extra edge of positive intent he was transmitting that day. By the time I'd caught up with him, he was already committed to an ambitious double which had paired up Timefighter with Paul Cole's Broken Hearted who was running in the Group 2 Prix Guillaume D'Ornano at Deauville. Timefighter's price had shortened dramatically though, and when the on-course bookmakers had finished pricing up, all I could see was 5/1.

Having first had a cautionary word with myself, I checked my basic instinct to get involved, calculating that the price was bound to drift. The reasoned, logical approach is one I like to use from time to time but it's not something on which I depend completely. As often, hunches hewn from deep down in the gut are just as likely to make me that little bit wealthier for a while.

On this occasion, I began to wish I'd travelled the more intuitive road instead. The price was simply cut again and I was left frustrated. Clearly, many among the assembled crowds knew more than was good for me about Timefighter. Just before the off the odds were 9/2 so I treated myself to a small supplementary bet. I wasn't prepared to surrender bragging rights to Miles quite so early in the piece. Although the bet had now been placed at that respectable, early-morning price,

I knew full well that in staking terms I'd played my hand poorly, and I've never liked wasting a decent deck.

In the race Timefighter was slowly away and did not appear to be going that well. The omens were not promising much in the way of glory. Miles was still, his ever-present binoculars fixed resolutely on the drama as it unfolded gradually before us. On the face of it, we'd been supplied with misinformation – and that grated. I prided myself on accurate research. As the field began to sweep across the side of the track, I felt a brief moment of quiet resignation, rather relieved that my own stake had been a relatively modest one.

Fleeting moments later however, in the final straight, the race was being turned on its head. The redoubtable Eddery, for so long the prince of punters nationwide, summoned up a typical piece of mastery. Timefighter was suddenly bursting forward with a new-found self-belief. His stride visibly quickened as his rider urged him forward relentlessly. Miles was now a man transformed. He bawled his encouragement with the same rhythmical certainty as Eddery's whip.

Now while I have never been wholly convinced that vocal contributions from the stands make much difference, there was absolutely no doubting the fact that Timefighter was now genuinely up with the pace. In the final furlong, with Eddery at his imperious best, he began to stay on strongly and appeared to level with the leaders in the very shadow of the finishing post. It was one of the closest finishes I had ever witnessed at the track – a four-way photograph between Timefighter,

Orient Line, Tertiary Zone and Queen's Bridge and one which was famously captured on the front page of the *Racing Post*.

Miles and I exchanged a momentary glance. He was still quivering in the after-shock of such a seismic contest. I recall he then merely shrugged. Both of us were speechless, both of us not daring to reassure the other. The thrill of it all though was unmistakable. Was it the tightest of finishes that had transfixed us or the staggering thought of just how much money was on the line? Everything hinged on one photograph.

Instinctively, we scampered down to the winners' enclosure in search of other opinions. The wait for the official result would obviously be an extensive one given the closeness of the finish. We'd both been in similar positions before but, for me, never had so much been resting on one, single outcome. It was agonising. Even Eddery's own confident demeanour didn't satisfy us completely. I don't know why. It usually did. But it was enough to persuade us to back our selection to win the verdict so we dashed back into the betting ring to take the best prices on offer.

After a painful delay the result was finally announced and we were smiling. Eddery's confident nod to Miles had not been misplaced. Our winnings could now be safely pouched. Miles even had the pleasure of collecting on his double because Broken Hearted delivered for him in France.

Three-year-old handicap races are tricky contests to solve, and have become more difficult over the years due to tighter handicapping. Whilst they may pose a challenging intellectual problem, they are not my idea of a good betting medium. There is a good reason that the majority of races sponsored by bookmakers are handicaps. However, the property that makes this type of race such a challenge (ie the normalising effect of the different weights carried) also has the effect of introducing a degree of uniformity across the race grade. This can be advantageous to some systematic techniques. For approaches employing draw-based methods, for example, and those relating speed to handicap ratings.

There can be an element of confusion concerning the relationship between handicap ratings and weight carried. A handicap mark is simply a convenient way of expressing the ability of one horse relative to another. For example, if two three-year-old colts were rated 87 and 97, the latter could be said to be 10lb superior to the former and in a handicap race would carry 10lb more weight. The ratings themselves do not determine the amount of weight to be carried, just the weight one horse will carry relative to another. Therefore, it would be possible for these two horses to be set to carry 8-04 and 9-00 in one race, and 8-11 and 9-07 in another contest on the same day. The absolute weight carried is determined by the rating of the highest rated horse in the race. In these two hypothetical contests the top-rated horse in the first race would be rated higher than the top-rated horse in the second race.

This is an important distinction and means that a horse carrying 9-07, for instance, is not necessarily badly handicapped, and an animal set to carry 8-04 is not guaranteed to be well handicapped. The weight carried by a horse simply reflects the overall strength of the race and the runner's perceived ability. Just because a Flat handicapper is set to carry 10-00 is no reason to assume it cannot win.

Timefighter carried 9-07 at Newbury and was running after finishing third in a stakes race. From the following table we can see that all runners in three-year-old handicap races which had been placed in a stakes event on their last run, have made a profit of 25p/£ at industry starting price over the five years covered by the analysis. And for runners carrying between 9-00 and 9-07 this profit increases to 55p/£, so maybe Timefighter was a good thing after all, even at industry starting price.

ANALYSIS OF RUNNERS IN THREE-YEAR-OLD HANDICAP RACES WHICH WERE PLACED ON THEIR LAST RUN IN A STAKES RACE

Weight Carried	Wins	Runs	Wins%	Profit*/£
9-08 ..10-00	2	9	22%	1.17
9-00 .. 9-07	17	132	13%	0.55
8-08 .. 8-13	5	55	9%	-0.16
8-00 .. 8-07	2	26	8%	-0.60
..7-13	0	2	0%	-1.00
All Runners	26	224	12%	0.25

* profit given to industry starting price

However, the degree of uniformity associated with these races is evident from the following tables which show the average profit/loss figures to starting price for all runners in three-year-old handicaps, illustrating the size of the problem faced by bettors.

ANALYSIS OF RUNNERS IN THREE-YEAR-OLD HANDICAP RACES BY WEIGHT CARRIED

Weight Carried	Wins	Runs	Wins%	Profit*/£
10-01+	0	4	0%	-1.00
9-08 ..10-00	98	523	19%	-0.21
9-00 .. 9-07	1678	13306	13%	-0.17
8-08 .. 8-13	809	8722	9%	-0.19
8-00 .. 8-07	327	5246	6%	-0.33
..7-13	27	622	4%	-0.29
All Runners	2939	28423	10%	-0.21

* profit given to industry starting price

Though the win rate seems highly correlated with weight carried, the average loss to bettors is remarkably consistent across the weight bands suggesting that this trend is fully accounted for in the starting price.

ANALYSIS OF RUNNERS IN THREE-YEAR-OLD HANDICAP RACES BY DAYS OFF THE TRACK

Days Off	Wins	Runs	Wins%	Profit*/£
1..7	286	2014	14%	-0.14
8..14	647	6228	10%	-0.27
15..28	1174	10651	11%	-0.15
29..60	466	5114	9%	-0.25
61..100	71	954	7%	-0.38
101+	295	3447	9%	-0.21
All Runners	2653	26394	10%	-0.21

* profit given to industry starting price

The "*Days Off*" table shows a similar pattern to the one represented in the weight analysis with the win rate increasing as the number of days off the track decreases, but again the loss figures remain stubbornly high for all groups.

ANALYSIS OF RUNNERS IN THREE-YEAR-OLD HANDICAP RACES BY STARTING PRICE

Starting Price	Wins	Runs	Wins%	Profit*/£
Odds On	124	196	63%	0.07
Ev - 2/1	397	1096	36%	-0.04
9/4 - 4/1	830	3913	21%	-0.12
9/2 - 6/1	472	3553	13%	-0.19
13/2-10/1	637	6485	10%	-0.11
11/1-16/1	309	6014	5%	-0.26
18/1-33/1	153	5198	3%	-0.26
40/1+	17	1968	1%	-0.55
All Runners	2418	27131	9%	-0.22

* profit given to industry starting price

The starting price analysis does suggest that some horses may be under bet, or overpriced. Naturally the success rate is closely linked to the starting price, but there is a marked difference in the range of profit and loss figures. For the long shots the loss is a staggering 55p/£ implying that these horses will offer no value at all to industry starting price. However those at the other end of the scale actually returned a profit over the five years. Backing all 196 odds-on shots would have made the bettor a 7p/£ profit to starting price, and those in the evens to 2/1 bracket lost just 4p/£.

As a note of caution, most of the profit for the odds on bets was recorded in the first two years of the analysis and since then they have only just broken even.

ANALYSIS OF RUNNERS IN THREE-YEAR-OLD HANDICAP RACES BY POSITION ON LAST RUN

Position LTO	Wins	Runs	Wins%	Profit*/£
Won	738	4394	17%	-0.18
2nd or 3rd	857	6120	14%	-0.15
Unplaced	1343	17854	8%	-0.23
All Runners	2938	28368	10%	-0.20

* profit given to industry starting price

This final table shows that finishing position on the latest start is a reasonable predictor of chance of success, and that those runners which made the frame on their most recent run tend to lose less. However they do still lose because this factor, and its relevance, is taken into account when the prices are determined.

Checking other factors is slightly more informative. Distance winners lose, on average 15p/£, beaten favourites lose 18p/£ and horses that have won previously on the same going have lost 21p/£. However, in the starting price table we could see that horses nearer the front of the market lost less per bet, with odds-on shots actually making a profit and this is reflected if we isolate the market leader. Over the five years of the analysis, the absolute favourites lost just 2p/£ which converts to a profit of 9p/£ from the 2629 bets at exchange prices before commission.

Another more surprising result is the return for course winners. The analysis showed that the 1,578 horses which were returning to a course they had previously won on, returned a loss of just 2p/£ to industry starting price which, due to the distribution with regard to prices, translated to a 20p/£ profit at exchange prices before commission. Admittedly 2010 was an exceptional year for these runners, boasting a profit of 63p/£ but even without those qualifiers a healthy profit would have been made. More worryingly for followers of this approach is that the bulk of the profit was produced by the longer priced runners, making it far less reliable than the favourite-based method.

While data-mining a particular race grade can produce a workable system, it is better, from a systems perspective, to take an idea and then use the data to develop it. The tables in this section indicate that there are data combinations which have produced good profits in the past, but without a sound, logical justification for why this is the case, it is difficult to be confident that they will continue to produce similar profits in the future.

Essentially, three-year-old handicaps are difficult races from which to make a long-term profit and, excluding draw-based methods, this is one race grade where my search for a winning system has so far not yielded the results I had hoped it would.

Chapter 7

Bring in the Experts

Betting was taking up much more of my time and without realising it I had become totally immersed in the sport. I watched every race shown on television, if not live then recorded, and Sara and I were racing most weekends. I was also taking time off work during the week to go to local meetings which stretched from Newton Abbot in the south west to Folkestone in the east and as far as York in the north.

One cold October day we made the 300-mile round trip to Exeter in the autumn half-term to watch Barnbrook Again win the Haldon Gold Cup, a race which has been immortalised by A J Dent's famous painting, "Autumn Campaigners", a copy of which still hangs above my desk at home as well as in the homes of many of our friends. Our evenings out were spent with racing friends, either those directly involved in the sport, or others with a deep interest in it, and all future engagements, be that holidays, day trips, or simple meetings, were arranged around the racing calendar. Very rarely was racing far from my next thought.

I was still employed by the PMB and in a relatively short space of time had rewritten all of the computer systems so that they were easier to maintain and run. The statistics department was gradually getting more efficient and each time we had a change of staff the number of hours offered to the prospective new employee was reduced. When I started in 1986 we had three full-time staff, by the end of 1989 we were down to 2.4, and even then there were times of the year when we were over-staffed so the statistics clerk would also work for other departments.

The potato crop is seasonal and so too is the collection and analysis of production data. The total area planted needed to be forecast then checked, along with the area of headlands (part of each field which is left unplanted to facilitate the movement of machinery). Once the crop reached maturity, daily yield assessments were recorded in order to more accurately forecast the total production of potatoes in Great Britain. Prices were monitored both at the farm gate and through the main retailers. The difference between these two sets of figures always surprised me: as a general rule the price of potatoes sold by the multiples (Tesco, Sainsbury's etc) was approximately double the price the producer received for them. Through the winter months national stock checks were made at the end of October, November and February as well as mid-January.

These censuses provided the board members with information regarding the volume of potatoes available after usage and waste, and stemmed back to the second world war when the PMB was first created. During the conflict it was important to have accurate supply statistics for all crops hence the need for such close monitoring. In fact many of the files we used in the office dated back to the 1930s and held type-written pages of data relating to the area planted to each variety as well as the yield per acre. Many of these files, to which we simply added the new printouts each season, were marked with a red "Secret" stamp on the front cover showing how important these figures were once deemed to be to the authorities. Post war the surveys and censuses were continued in order to give an idea of the supply/demand balance and whether any intervention strategies were required.

Import and export data, supplied by Customs and Excise, was the other component on the balance sheet and it was notoriously inaccurate. As well as mis-classifications, such as bananas labelled as potatoes, there were also problems with the country of origin. In one notable example Great Britain apparently took possession of 300,000 tonnes of potatoes exported from the Vatican City. I realise that His Papal Holiness has an interest in many things, but I was unaware that he was such a prolific potato grower.

These data were reported to the Ministry of Agriculture, Fisheries and Food (MAFF) at four points in the year, and it was my task to attend the meetings in London and present the latest forecasts. At my first meeting in 1986, I was surprised to be told that it was no longer a requirement for visitors to wear hats so my attire was acceptable, but that this had been the case in years gone by. This was another quirky civil service regulation which I found hard to believe but was assured was true; I remain unconvinced.

Even though I could attend hat-free, the meetings did still

disrupt my betting. At the time it was almost impossible to get a mobile phone signal in Westminster, and using an office telephone to place bets would have resulted in instant dismissal for the civil servant whose phone was used. Consequently I had to negotiate an early start to the meetings with ministry staff (normally 10am) so that I could hurry to the nearest bookmakers to place any bets my systems had highlighted. Fortunately the civil servants were aware of my betting schedule and were very obliging regarding meeting times.

By 1990 the repetitive nature of the position I held was getting difficult to cope with and I needed a new challenge. Leaving the PMB was an option I considered, but I finally decided to apply to take a Master of Philosophy degree course at Oxford Brookes University. MPhil degrees are purely research-based. There is no need to attend regular lectures or tutorials, so they are better suited to part-time students with work commitments. This meant that I could carry on working at the PMB and research for the degree at the same time. My chosen area of study was expert systems, with specific reference to the application of expert systems to forecasting. A key aspect of MPhil degrees is that they tend to be more practical than, say, PhDs, so it was necessary to find a domain to which I could apply the results of my academic work. Naturally there was only ever going to be one choice: horseracing.

My decision to start the course coincided with the arrival of a new mainframe computer at the PMB. Reportedly costing over £1m, the Unisys machine could compete with most other computers in the country in terms of storage and processing, but needed a temperature-controlled environment in which to function.

On the day it was installed I watched the components being wheeled into the specially converted room on sack trolleys, and at one point asked what was in a box which stood four feet high and was about two feet square at its base. "Hard drive," was the reply, "one gig." A whole gigabyte of storage, at that time, was incredible; we'd never use that much storage I thought. Of course eventually we did, and by today's computers the machine was not particularly impressive. The laptop on which I am typing, for instance, has over 100GB of storage, and that is nearly full!

A condition of the MPhil course was the participation of two mentors, one from the university and one from my place of work. The university allocated John Nealon, and at work I approached Dr Stuart Walker, the head of the computing department. Fortunately he agreed and that gave me access to the mainframe under his guidance. All I needed now was a set of data to work on, and for this I turned to Raceform.

James de Wesselow, the managing director at Raceform, seemed keen to help me with the research and could no doubt see the commercial possibilities if my work was successful. However, I was surprised to learn that the Raceform office in Compton, near Newbury, did not hold the formbook data used by their very popular, but at the time error packed,

Computer Raceform. It was all sourced from Weatherbys.

Acting as racing's administrators, Weatherbys was established over 200 years ago, and within their offices Raceform had a small department which produced the weekly issues of the formbook and kept the software database up to date. James arranged a visit for Stuart and me, and within a few days we were in possession of boxes of large tapes holding the information I needed. Stuart loaded these onto the PMB's mainframe and, after a little pre-processing, I was ready to start analysing the results of ten years of Flat races run in Great Britain.

As much as I wanted to start testing and developing systems for my own betting, I could not lose sight of the aim of my research which was to examine the application of expert systems to forecasting.

Expert systems, the most common application of artificial intelligence in the 1980s, are knowledge-based systems, although the converse is not necessarily true. They employ the solution methods used by human experts in narrow, well-defined domains to solve problems. There are two main components to an expert system: a knowledge base and an inference engine.

As the name implies, the knowledge base contains all the knowledge items the system developer has been able to distil from the experts and the available literature. This is where the power of an expert system lays, its detailed, in-depth, apparent understanding of a specific domain. As a rule, the knowledge base is kept separate from the other parts of the system, ie from routines to handle the user interface, and it is written in a clear, readable fashion, which makes it more accessible to the operators and simplifies the process of adding new knowledge. Thus, the knowledge of an expert system can continue to be increased or modified after the official end of the development stage.

This is not always the case with conventional computer programs. The inference engine controls the system and may be said to perform the reasoning. It adopts a suitable reasoning strategy, such as backward or forward chaining, to infer conclusions for the input query. The choice of inferencing procedure will depend on the nature of the problem and the chosen mode of knowledge representation. In many cases though, a combination of techniques will be used.

An important decision in the development of an expert system is the selection of a format for representing the knowledge. There are several established formats, the most common of which are rules, frames and semantic networks. For the horseracing system I was developing, in order to demonstrate the usefulness of expert systems with regard to forecasting, I chose a rule-based representation since it more closely mirrored the methods employed by expert race analysts. However, both frames and semantic networks could also be applicable to this problem.

The development of a knowledge-based, or expert,

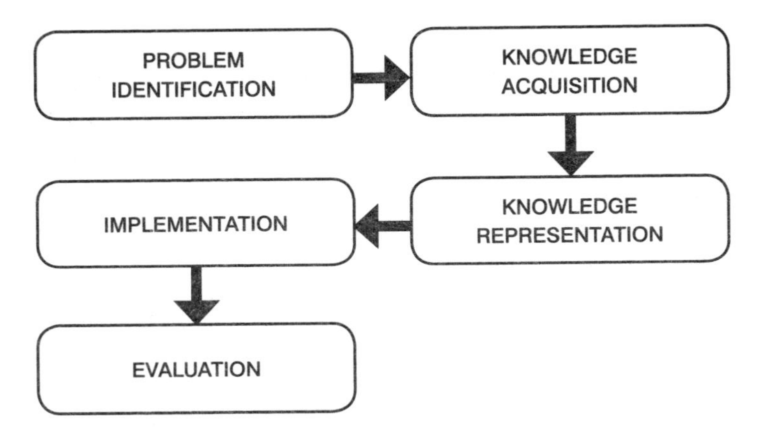

system can be considered as having five stages (illustrated). The initial exercise is one of problem identification. The project aims need to be clearly stated and the key problem characteristics identified. This will always constitute the first stage of any system development project. Due to the nature and complexity of tasks addressed by knowledge-based systems, the knowledge acquisition phase, stage two, will overlap with the remaining three stages and will possibly be returned to after the testing phase. During this critical process the knowledge engineer (system developer) will attempt to extract, from a range of sources, the knowledge required by the system.

It is generally accepted that the knowledge acquisition phase is one of the primary bottlenecks in the development of knowledge-based systems. While much of the knowledge required to build the system may be contained in available literature, the main source of input will often be human experts so I needed to interview some of racing's top analysts.

James de Wesselow was able to help again and he arranged for me to spend a day working with Mel Collier at the *Racing Post*'s offices, and also to interview David Dickinson and John de Moraville, now both BHA handicappers, as well as Charles Fawcus of the *Daily Mirror*.

It was interesting to learn how these experts approached the problem of forecasting the result of a horserace, and each employed a different solution method. Collier only had six races to analyse every day when putting together the Spotlight paragraphs for the *Racing Post* and he went into a great deal of detail for each runner, including examining in-depth trainer patterns. Charles Fawcus, who had to tip in every race of the day for the *Daily Mirror*, had limited time to examine the form in detail, so he checked for key factors and combined these with stable-based information. John de Moraville adopted a more ratings-based approach and made use of Raceform's own private handicap data in order to make his predictions for the *Daily Express*. Raceform's David Dickinson was not a tipster but a handicapper. In the interview he demonstrated how to construct a handicap based on previous race results, then told me that for his own betting he was a keen user of draw biases. While all of the interviews were very informative it was this reference to the draw that I found most intriguing.

I had read references to the effect of the draw in many

publications, but nowhere had I seen a detailed analysis of the tracks. Normally comments were restricted to "high stalls favoured", or similar. I wanted a numerical breakdown by stall number for every race distance at every racecourse in Great Britain, and thanks to Weatherbys I had the means to produce it.

However I soon found out that analysing the draw is not as straightforward as I first thought, and it took a huge amount of paper to complete the work, as the computer operations staff were keen to point out to me each time I went to the computer room to collect another printout.

Simply analysing all races is not the most effective way to determine a draw effect. It is more informative to restrict the analysis to handicaps. The ability range of the runners in these contests is normalised by the allocation of different weights by the BHA handicappers, therefore only a small external effect makes a noticeable change to the result of the race. In non-handicaps the ability range is likely to be much wider, and even with the best draw of the race and a ten lengths start, a large proportion of the runners would still fail to win. In other words, the draw will not, in most cases, be a significant determining factor in non-handicaps, the crucial element being the ability of the horses. A similar argument can be applied to nurseries, although not to quite the same extent. Less exposed two-year-old horses are exceptionally difficult to handicap and therefore the differing abilities will not be accounted for as well as they are for older horses.

As well as restricting the analysis to non-juvenile handicap races, a further distinction is required to complete the analysis, namely the position of the stalls. The position of the stalls on the track will determine, to some extent, the part of the track the horses will race on. So when the stalls are on the inside of a left-handed track, the runner from stall one will race closest to the inner running rail; with the stalls on the outside of the track the horse drawn in stall one may well be running down the centre of the track.

A simple analysis of win rate by stall number for a specific stall position is informative but does disguise certain characteristics such as the field-size effect. For instance, a horse drawn 16 will have at least 15 other horses to beat (excluding non-runners), whereas a horse drawn in stall four may only face three opponents, and consequently a better chance of success. To account for this effect it is necessary to compare the win rate to the expected win rate. Since the draw is made randomly, one method for calculating this figure is to take the reciprocal of the number of runners in each race and aggregate these fractions. So, as an example, in a ten-runner race each stall would have an expectation of 1/10 and in a 20-runner race this figure would reduce to 1/20.

Given the results of five races featuring 8, 10, 12, 14 and 16 runners over a certain distance at a particular track, we can calculate the expected number of winners for stall one as:

$$1/8 + 1/10 + 1/12 + 1/14 + 1/16 = 0.44$$

An advantage ratio can then be calculated by dividing the

actual number of winners from the stall by the expected number of winners. A system can then be constructed using this ratio, for example:

Back all horses with a draw ratio > 1.5

So, for the example given, if the five races produced two winners from stall 1, the advantage ratio would be:

2/0.44 = 4.5

The result in this example, 4.5, is greater than the ratio in our rule, but basing a system on just five observations is not recommended, so in this case I would not follow these runners until the sample increased to a sufficient size and then only if a significant draw ratio was maintained.

For races where the highest stall number is against the rail a small adjustment to the analysis is required: the stall needs to be considered in relation to a constant base stall. The easiest way to do this is to adjust the stall numbers themselves. Therefore, in a 20-runner race stall 20 becomes stall zero, stall 19 becomes stall one and so on. And in an eight runner race, stall eight becomes stall zero, stall seven becomes stall one etc. The resulting analysis is then comparable to that for races where the lowest stall is against the rail.

The main criticism of this approach concerns the use of the reciprocal of the number of runners to derive the expected number of winners. However this is easily justified because the large sample size and random allocation of draw will result in the winners, on unbiased tracks, being uniformly distributed across the stalls without favour to any particular position. Consequently using a constant in this respect is valid. However it is important not to use variables such as starting price to set the expectation. Though starting price is representative of the chance of success in many cases it is not possible to be certain that it takes no account for the draw effect and hence may be a biased measure.

Using this approach I quickly amassed a selection of tracks which I thought possessed biases sufficient to return a long-term profit and started following them. My bank started increasing and I realised that I had found an excellent system.

However, while preparing for year two of following the draw method, I lost sight of the aim of the approach which was to identify reliable draw biases and found many courses which appeared to exhibit potentially profitable biases, but which in reality did not. I had become blinded by the numbers, and now had a portfolio of tracks to follow that included many which were the result of randomness rather than a true bias.

There are several ways in which the draw can affect the outcome of a race. Firstly, moisture is not necessarily retained uniformly across the width of the course, consequently the horses running on the softer, or slower, side will be at a considerable disadvantage. Naturally, non-uniform moisture retention is especially apparent on cambered tracks with the lower part of the course retaining water for a longer period of time.

Such variability in the ground conditions becomes more significant in sprint races where horses tend not to group together. Over longer distances the runners tend to bunch together soon after the start thus minimising the effect of the softer ground. Secondly, horses often run better when positioned close to a running rail. The rail prevents the horse from wandering across the track (at least in one direction), keeping its path to the line straighter. And thirdly, on round courses, horses drawn on the inside will benefit from taking the shortest route from starting stall to finishing line. All of these factors can influence the outcome of a race.

Once I had identified stalls which satisfied my rule (given previously), I should have checked that there was a reason for the bias, instead I merely trusted the data and it caused me to lose heavily. It did teach me a good lesson about following systems though.

The following year I went back to my core set of tracks, evaluated them again, checked the course maps, and even watched videos in an attempt to identify those with a true bias. I could have applied a range of statistical techniques to verify the data, but on a stall-by-stall basis the size of the sample was relatively small and I believed the result could be misleading so I adopted the observational path. The tracks that remained after this cull were those which had been profitable in my first year of following the draw and most will be well known to readers: Sandown 5F, York 10F, Beverley 5F, Chester 5-7F, Folkestone 9F, and my most profitable course Ripon 6F.

Keeping to the established courses returned good profits over the next couple of years for win bets and also Computer Straight Forecast (CSF) and Tricast bets. However an unwanted external influence was to severely curtail my profits. Bookmakers had also spotted the biases and decided that an amendment was required to their most lucrative of bets in order to preserve their huge margin of profitability. Therefore changes to the calculation of the CSF and Tricast were put in place so that the payouts were reduced when horses from neighbouring stalls filled the first few positions. These two bets already had massive inbuilt over-rounds in the layers' favour, and these additional alterations made them even poorer value so I simply stopped placing these bets and concentrated on win-only wagers.

Other factors were also coming into play which did not help my cause. The draw biases were beginning to get known and the value was gradually disappearing; furthermore racecourse staff were making changes to the tracks in order to nullify the biases. Clearly there was little they could do when the bias was determined by a bend in the course, but for biases based on irrigation systems and drainage it was possible to make changes. As I mentioned previously, environmental changes such as these can have a devastating effect on the best of systems and over the next few years the number of profitable tracks declined.

In spite of these changes, my favourite course was performing well for me again in 1994. For all non-juvenile handicaps staged over six furlongs at Ripon, I would customarily back the horses drawn in stalls one and two, regardless of any other factor. This approach had returned good profits in previous years, so I put my faith in Lady Sheriff and Kid Ory on 25 May 1994.

The race was run in the evening and the start-time clashed (inconveniently for some) with the very latest episode of one of the nation's perennial favourites, *Coronation Street*. In those days, the soaps still held their charm for Sara – not to mention several million other regular partakers. Things may be a bit different these days but back then, the seductive allure of this timeless TV treat could never be lightly dismissed. As a teacher in the mid-1990s, life was relatively straightforward. A mere 50 hours per week would leave her ample time to lounge in front of what Basil Fawlty would have doubtless termed a "few aimless thrills". Nowadays, still dutifully playing her part in the same profession, 60 to 70 hours seems to be the minimum required. Unfortunately, that does of course put those same television highlights out of reach.

The actual set which we owned at that point, used to allow teletext pages to be selected and frozen, so I remember locating the exact betting page I required for the race and vitally pressing "hold" just before Britain's longest running soap was due to hit our screens once again. During the commercial break, admittedly with no warning, I suddenly switched channels back to BBC1 from ITV and re-selected the teletext button for an update. I sensed Sara's unspoken annoyance at the prospect of her missing some crucial moments of the unfolding drama. Seconds later, having tremulously re-selected the "hold" button, the result I'd been seeking flashed up before my eager eyes. Kid Ory had won at 20/1.

I smiled like I always try to smile on a productive day – understatedly – and casually remarked: "That's a nice result." And so as not to spoil the impact of my news, I quickly converted the viewing back to Weatherfield.

"Did you back that one then?" enquired Sara rather disinterestedly. To give her proper credit for once, throughout all our high spots and quite a few of our more forgettable forages into the betting market, she has usually been prepared to show an interest, even when she would much rather have allowed herself the chance to opt out and fully relax. I know I'm very lucky in this sense and one day I'll tell her.

"Yes, I backed it," I replied, deliberately offering no further explanation and risking her wrath for forcing her to postpone her precious soap-time a little bit longer for the sake of a slightly longer conversation. There was a further short pause. I can be quite irritating when I've got good news. I accept that.

"How much?" she asked.

"Just £100 to win." I knew the numbers wouldn't be beyond the secondary maths specialist but I couldn't help but make her calculate the jackpot for herself. I was drawing every ounce of drama out of a real-life situation at the expense of the make-believe stuff she would have rather had left uninterrupted. Sara feigned her own brand of detachment. She was always more than a match for me in these types of games. Another pause followed, far longer than it would have taken her to do the numbers.

"So you won £2,000 then?"

I affirmed this truth with minimal fuss. I suppose I wanted Sara to think I would be achieving this on an increasingly regular basis and that this was what she could come to expect. Eyes still glued to Rita Fairclough and friends, Sara's reaction was suitably lukewarm. Though I usually detected a hint of pride and pleasure behind the mask when the win was a more significant one, Sara was not about to profit from the win and she knew it.

"I don't expect I'll see any of it," she stated matter-of-factly.

As far as cold-shoulders can be measured in hindsight, I was perched alongside a particularly icy one for the rest of that evening. But Sara's curmudgeonly reaction was strictly blameless of course – a quality, I've learned to accept, which is common to most wives and especially my own. The £2,000, as she fully realised, was heading unerringly to my betting bank to resurface on another betting day. It would have no frivolous purpose upon which she could feast her imagination. She did get to enjoy the remainder of *Coronation Street* though!

Since then, as the wins have become more frequent in their regularity, my betting account has been more readily accessible for all sorts of essential, and slightly less essential purchases. I've certainly softened since my terribly protective, do-not-touch, early days. It was hard for Sara to understand and I was not clever at explaining matters, often with more spin than your average cabinet minister's fresh policy statement. At that stage of my betting life I viewed every penny won as an extra penny to re-invest in a bigger, more exciting project. I was building foundations and I knew that any type of permanent construction is careful, serious work. These days, it's a little different. Sara's only recently benefited to the tune of a new car. It's been a long road and her patience, like that new car, has had to be fully tested on more than one occasion.

Over the next few years the profitability of the draw system declined and now I no longer follow it to such an extent but there are still some tracks where it is worth checking and building into any forecasting models.

> Bath 5F (high); Beverley 5F (low); Brighton 7-8F (high); Chepstow 8F (low); Lingfield (turf) 5-6F (high); Newcastle 5-7F (high); Sandown 5F (low).

If you decide to form your own draw-based method then there are a few other points to consider. The main problem with systems based on the draw is the success rate. Such methods generally produce one winner every five bets, and this low strike rate means that long losing runs are inevitable.

Fortunately it is possible to improve the strike rate by considering other factors, such as the price the horse started at for its last race, the current price, and running styles. In handicap races, the type in which the draw produces the best return, there is a strong correlation between the success rate and the starting price of the horse for its latest race. The longer the price the less likely the horse is to win. So in order to increase the success rate of the system, selections that started at long odds for their latest runs, such as 33/1 or higher, can be omitted. Naturally this will lead to missing winners on occasion, so as an alternative to ignoring these selections completely, the stake can be reduced and a graduated staking plan introduced.

Another key element is the number of runners in the race. In very small fields the effect of the bias will not be so crucial. For instance, in a four-runner five-furlong sprint at Haydock with the stalls on the stands' side, all the runners could be considered to be benefiting from the draw, with the poorest drawn horse (in stall 1) being only a few yards from the favoured running rail. In this instance there is no advantage to be had. For draw followers the larger the field the better, since an increasingly greater proportion of the runners will be suffering from a poor draw, yet their presence in the race will help to inflate the price of the better-drawn horses. From an analysis of the data it has been found that only races with seven or more runners should be considered for betting purposes.

One further consideration for betting on the draw is the running style of the selection. It is important in sprints and races which are run on the turn in the first few furlongs to select horses with good early pace. A slow-starting animal can lose a good position within a matter of strides and then have to round part or the entire field to have any chance of winning, completely negating the positive effect of the draw. Naturally, it is difficult to tell whether the selection has a good early pace. In the absence of inexpensive, easily available, sectional timing, the next best guide is the comment-in-running associated with the animal's recent runs. The comments found in the formbook are particularly useful and the key words to check for include: held up, started slowly, missed break, always behind, outpaced early. It is good policy to avoid horses which have received these, or similar comments on recent runs.

Chapter Eight

All-Age Handicaps and the Worst Bet in Racing

By 1992 my research was drawing to a close. All of the interviews with the horseracing experts had been concluded, transcribed, and the key facts distilled. These, along with many other rules extracted from racing books, had been assembled into a knowledge base. An applicable reasoning strategy had been established and the expert system could now process Group and Listed races. After a period of testing it was ready for use so Raceform set up a dedicated tipping line called Raceform Gold and the service went live.

I was still betting on various system qualifiers including the juveniles to follow and the draw method, also any information-based selections from Miles and the Forster stable. In addition I was providing selections via Raceform Gold, or to be completely accurate, the expert system was providing the selections. But more importantly I had to complete the write-up for the MPhil. This was not easy. Although I had many sources of information to draw on, such as academic papers, books, and the results of my own research, compiling it into a single 20,000 word script was particularly challenging.

My supervisor, John Nealon, was a vital ally and we spent

many a long hour at the university discussing the content of the thesis and re-drafting chapters in the quest for what seemed a rather elusive sense of perfection.

During one of these quite intensive sessions we were memorably interrupted by a knock at the door. A serious-looking woman, of uncertain middle age, entered warily. In the gentlest of tones and with the finest diction she could possibly muster, she wondered whether she had, "correctly located the intelligent systems department". John confirmed that she had. Rather randomly, our mysterious visitor then probed us as to whether we thought an intelligent computer system might be utilised to analyse the works of William Shakespeare.

"Of course it could," we replied, almost in unison. Entirely unsolicited, the lady continued to volunteer additional information with respect to her lifelong devotion to the Bard's classic catalogue and explained that she wished to analyse it in depth using the latest technology.

"How would you go about it?" she enquired with a slightly manic fervour. Summoning up a highly impressive level of forbearance, considering we had a not insignificant task of our own to fulfil, John began to explain that we'd first need to have a precise and profound understanding of the actual type of analysis she was looking to conduct, so that an appropriate system could be designed accordingly. From that point, he added, we would need to type a selected play into the machine and generate a report.

At this point, our dogged interrogator quite abruptly cut off John and ventured with incredible sincerity: "So the computer does not actually know Shakespeare then?" Her query was so naive we might have mocked her mercilessly but she was so earnest in her manner it would have been too disrespectful, however tempting.

"No," John replied through gritted teeth, tethering up his natural instincts quite remarkably, "Why would it?" Bearing in mind this was a pre-internet project, it was unlikely that databases like these would exist, ones which would already comprise such easily accessible information.

"Well, I thought the computer was supposed to be intelligent," she continued in what was now growing into quite a haughty tone. "I had assumed that it would know Shakespeare." Upon which statement, she bustled out of the room.

To this visitor of ours, a system or perhaps even a human being would not be considered intelligent if he, she or it didn't know Shakespeare. That was her own acid test – her personal definition perhaps but, to us, it was a strictly limited, simplistic view and, true to the Stratford playwright's incomparable genius, one which had expertly blended the comic with the particularly tragic!

Many computer systems have been developed that are labelled intelligent. For instance, chess programs are now capable of beating even the very best players. In 1997, for example, the IBM supercomputer, Deep Blue, defeated the world chess champion Gary Kasparov. However, any assessment of machine intelligence is dependent upon the definition of the word intelligent. It has been argued that, in the main, programmed solutions simply reflect, but do no possess, the intelligence of a human. Since the programs do not produce the solution method themselves they cannot be thought of as intelligent.

Other definitions simply require a system to exhibit a level of understanding to be labelled intelligent. In this instance, understanding implies a depth of knowledge about a specific issue from which, given a reasoning strategy, a conclusion or explanation not necessarily held within the system, may be derived. In other words, an internet search engine may be able to find the answer to specific questions posed, but for it to be truly intelligent, it would have to take this information and form an answer to a different question, for which a ready-made solution is not available.

This is illustrated by John Searle's *Chinese Room* problem. This thought experiment concerns two people, one of whom only speaks English and the other Chinese. Given a book of Chinese phrases they should be able to communicate with the English speaker taking the written Chinese expressions, comparing them to those listed in the phrase book, and then providing the relevant response. The English speaker can be substituted by a computer and the phrase book by a program. Although the conversation could still continue, most probably much more quickly, the computer possesses no understanding of Chinese, merely responding in a pre-programmed fashion, therefore cannot be considered to be intelligent.

For the Shakespeare analogy, someone who was able to quote references from the plays may be considered knowledgeable, but a person who could interpret the meanings of the plays would be thought to be intelligent.

The expert system I developed contained domain knowledge in the form of rules, plus an inferencing strategy which generated a forecast for each race presented. However it would probably be classified as knowledgeable rather than intelligent due to the restricted nature of the output it could produce.

Once I had completed the thesis it was assessed by an external examiner and in 1993 I was awarded a Master of Philosophy degree by the University. Though I was pleased to have satisfactorily completed the degree, I had lost the most interesting part of my working life and was faced with the prospect of more potato stock censuses, field area surveys and inaccurate import data to query, without the welcome interruptions caused by researching expert systems. One benefit was that it did give me more time to devote to horseracing and my search for profitable systems.

Although I was not keen on betting in handicaps (except for the draw method), in the early 1990s this race classification made up almost half of all races run, and by ignoring them I was severely restricting the number of potentially profitable systems I could implement. Nowadays this race type constitutes approximately three-quarters of all-age races staged in Great Britain and as a result demands even more attention from bettors hoping to make a decent return from the sport.

As mentioned earlier, handicaps are difficult to solve. The BHA currently employs a team of handicappers to set the ratings (or handicap marks) for each horse with the aim of producing races in which all horses, regardless of their ability, have equal chances of success. For many racing fans it is disappointing that a sport, initially designed to test the relative merits of horses over various distances, is now dominated by races that simply determine which runners are under or over assessed by the official handicapper.

The handicap marks are equivalent to form ratings and are a convenient way of expressing the ability of one horse relative to another. Handicap marks are expressed in pounds, therefore if two three-year-old colts were rated 104 and 108, the latter could be said to be four pounds superior to the former. In order to satisfy the stated aim of handicap races the better horses are penalised by giving them more weight to carry. So if these two horses met one would carry four pounds more weight.

Handicap ratings are adjusted after each race, with the mark of the winner increased on most occasions, and those horses thought to be too high in the handicap, based on the race performance, reduced. In order to assess whether a horse has run to its current handicap mark, the race is examined in detail and normally a benchmark horse is determined. This horse is deemed to have run to a specific mark and is normally a well-exposed, consistent runner. The other horses are then assessed with respect to this runner and their ratings adjusted accordingly.

The basis of the handicap adjustments is the distance, in horse lengths, between the horses at the finish of a race, converted to pounds (weight) using a scale based on the race distance. This weight scale can be approximated by the following formula:

$$\text{pounds (weight)} = \frac{\text{distance beaten in lengths} \times 15}{\text{race distance (f)}}$$

Thus if horse A beats horse B by two lengths in a five furlong race (both carrying the same weight) the superiority in pounds would be estimated at approximately 6lbs (ie 2 x 15 ÷ 5). For the same distance between the two horses in a 12 furlong race the superiority would be 2½lbs. This conversion is given in the *Distance To Weight Approximate* table.

DISTANCE TO WEIGHT APPROXIMATION

Race distance (f)	5f	6f	7f	8f	10f	12f	14f
Pounds per length	3	2.5	2.1	1.9	1.5	1.2	1.1

This conversion provides a basis for calculating the weight

adjustments, but the final weight rise/reduction is determined by the handicapper and can vary substantially from race to race, depending on the handicapper's assessment of the differences in ability between the runners. For example, although a horse may win by only one length, the manner of the victory may result in the handicapper basing its future rating on a win equivalent to, say, four lengths. This can give rise to disagreements between the handicappers and trainers who feel their horses have been harshly treated.

However the process does not take into account the time of the race, so it is likely that a horse would receive the same increase whether the race was run at a fast or slow pace. At the time I was investigating these races this appeared to be a weakness in the procedure and I decided to attempt to find a systematic method to exploit it.

The speed a race is run at is determined by its distance, the condition of the ground and the quality of the runners. Naturally, longer races take more time to run than shorter events; it is more difficult to run quickly on softer going; and if the horses are simply not very good then the race time is unlikely to be particularly impressive. Though the effect of these three factors is obvious, the race time is also dependent on the number of runners in the race. The fastest-run juvenile races, for example, are often the large field events such as the Weatherbys Super Sprint held at Newbury. A large field guarantees a strong pace throughout the race which inevitably leads to a good finishing time.

This being the case I reasoned that horses which won large-field handicaps may be under assessed for their next run and consequently could be value bets if they reappeared in another handicap. I ran the analysis at work and the results were encouraging for races with more than 20 runners, so the Hcap21 system was added to my portfolio of methods.

While the Hcap21 system worked well, the two main drawbacks were the number of bets and the win rate. Both were on the low side. Since the method was part of a set of systems I used, the number of bets per year was not such a big issue, though it did make validating the method less reliable. However low win rates are always difficult to deal with from the psychological perspective. Such systems often encounter long losing runs and it is easy to assume the system has stopped working during one of these phases, when in reality the poor run is merely a result of statistical randomness.

I ran the system for a few years and it did provide some good winners. The most memorable was Face North in the Royal Hunt Cup. Reg Akehurst's runner had previously won the Victoria Cup (25 runners) at Ascot in April, then returned to the course for the Royal meeting two months later to take the 32-runner handicap by half-a-length at a starting price of 25/1. This success qualified him as a system bet for his next handicap, but this time he found Fraam too good in the Golden Mile at Goodwood and was beaten a neck into second place. The fact that the Hcap21 method returned a profit, highlighted a potential weakness in the handicapping approach which could be possible to exploit more fully with a comprehensive speed-based approach.

ANALYSIS OF THE HCAP21 SYSTEM BY YEAR

Year	Wins	Runs	Wins%	Profit*/£
2005	3	15	21%	0.96
2006	0	17	0%	-1.00
2007	3	14	17%	0.19
2008	0	9	0%	-1.00
2009	3	14	23%	0.46
2010	3	16	19%	0.79
2011	2	14	14%	0.26
2012	4	24	17%	1.38
All Runners	18	123	15%	0.38

* profit given to exchange prices recorded at off time

Obviously a method that only finds a dozen bets per year is not going to make anyone rich, but it is good to see that it is still making a profit. While I remember the method finding more qualifiers in the early 1990s, I still needed to add more handicap systems to my portfolio.

As a general rule the more times a horse has raced, the more likely it is to be accurately handicapped and as a result the harder it is for it to win. These horses either need to find a degree of improvement to beat the handicap, or perform poorly for a period of time, resulting in a lowering of their handicap marks, then make a return to form. While it is possible to identify patterns in handicap performances which can be used to form systems for these experienced horses, it is easier to focus on the other set of runners, namely those which have been lightly raced.

In order to qualify for a handicap mark horses need to have either won a race or run at least three times. So it is possible for a horse to run in a handicap after just one or two races. These runners are particularly difficult to handicap since they are still improving and have raced only in non-handicap company. The process of identifying a benchmark horse in non-handicap events, around which to base the handicap ratings, is more difficult given that the majority of runners which have raced will probably not be rated and will also be lightly raced. It is these less exposed, difficult-to-rate runners which we can hopefully exploit in terms of a system.

Taking all-age handicaps (ie those not restricted to just juveniles or three-year-olds) as the base data set, then analysing by run number produces the following results for a five year period:

ANALYSIS OF ALL-AGE HANDICAP RACES BY RUN NUMBER

Run Number	Wins	Runs	Wins%	Profit*/£
2nd Run	27	270	10%	0.07
3rd Run	62	458	14%	-0.22
4th Run	162	1847	9%	-0.43
5th Run	226	2203	10%	-0.17
6th+ Run	7434	81379	9%	-0.21
All Runners	7911	86157	9%	-0.21

* profit given to industry starting price

For an industry starting price, the 7p/£ return for horses on their second career start is quite respectable, however this profit depends entirely on two very long-priced runners and it is unlikely to be repeated. As mentioned previously the horses which are most difficult to handicap accurately are those running after competing in non-handicap races. Isolating these gives the following analysis:

ANALYSIS OF ALL-AGE HANDICAP RACES BY RUN NUMBER FOR HORSES RUNNING AFTER COMPETING IN A NON-HANDICAP EVENT

Run Number	Wins	Runs	Wins%	Profit*/£
2nd Run	17	114	15%	0.82
3rd Run	35	212	17%	-0.03
4th Run	88	1349	7%	-0.54
5th Run	34	402	9%	-0.35
6th+ Run	402	6654	6%	-0.30
All Runners	576	8731	7%	-0.32

* profit given to industry starting price

As expected those making their second or third start perform best both in terms of success rate and profit. In fact these could form a system themselves with 52 winners from 326 runners and a level stake profit at starting price of 27p/£. However an analysis by year shows two very poor periods and the overall profile has an erratic look. Taking just those runners which won their last start produces the following results by year using the exchange prices to calculate the profit figures: 46 winners from 215 bets and a level stake profit at off time exchange prices of 39p/£.

Again there are not many bets, but each year was profitable and the sample contained no winner priced over 30.0. Furthermore restricting bets to horses priced at no more than 10.0 would have produced a profit of 26p/£ from over 100 bets showing a degree of uniformity across the price ranges.

Even though we started with a logical reason for expecting a profit, namely less exposed horses running after competing in a non-handicap, this type of data mining can produce systems that look good on paper, but fail to perform when implemented simply due to the data-mining process itself. Consequently they need to be thoroughly tested before any money is risked. Methods for validating systems are given later in this text and should be used to validate this or any other system before it is implemented.

One way a handicapper can improve on recent form is when encountering a different set of race conditions. These may take the form of a race distance and going state that the horse has met previously and performed well on, or they may be completely new to the animal in which case determining whether they will be suitable or not is more difficult. The previous system, for instance, is essentially based on a change of conditions, specifically the move from non-handicap to handicap races. While the method has the potential to be profitable, there are other ways to exploit this particular feature and the most obvious is to examine win rates and profitability by trainer.

Some trainers seem more adept at preparing horses for their first handicap race and as a result have enjoyed a profitable period over the last few years. The following list presents trainers that have had a good record with their non-juvenile handicap debutants on turf: Andrew Balding, Hughie Morrison, Luca Cumani, Amanda Perrett, and Richard Fahey. From the data it appears that horses from some of the more powerful stables are under priced early in the day because the layers are not prepared to take any chances. However, if these prices then drift the horse eventually becomes a value bet. For horses that have drifted in price during the day I would also add runners from the John Gosden and Sir Michael Stoute stables.

Fillies should be treated very carefully on their handicap debut run. In recent years over 3,500 have made the transition from non-handicap events and these have returned a loss of 36p/£ to industry starting price, which compares to a loss of 21p/£ for colts and geldings. Even at exchange prices these fillies make significant loss, 19p/£ over the same period.

Another interesting feature which became apparent while I was analysing handicap race data, was the high correlation between the win rate and the price the horse started at for its last race, which was discussed with respect to the draw-based methods in the previous chapter. Obviously there is a high correlation between success rates and starting price, but the connection also extends to the price the horse started on for its latest run which is more useful to a systems player. The following table shows this feature for all-age handicaps:

ANALYSIS OF ALL-AGE HANDICAP RACES BY STARTING PRICE ON LATEST RUN

Starting Price LTO	Wins	Runs	Wins%	Profit*/£
Odds On	95	483	20%	-0.06
Ev - 2/1	402	2605	15%	-0.17
9/4 - 4/1	1498	10987	14%	-0.14
9/2 - 6/1	1265	11379	11%	-0.22
13/2-10/1	2064	20866	10%	-0.17
11/1-16/1	1451	18655	8%	-0.24
18/1-33/1	933	15480	6%	-0.24
40/1+	203	5702	4%	-0.35

* profit given to industry starting price

Such a high degree of correlation implies that this attribute of an animal's form could be useful for generating systems as well as forecasting models and odds lines. However the starting price is not merely based on the runner's ability relative to its opponents, it is also influenced by the number of runners in the race. For it to be most effective in a model this needs to be accounted for. The simplest way to do this is to divide the price the horse started at last time out by the number of runners in the race to give a Last Race Price Ratio (LRPR). For example, if a runner had a 5/1 starting price on its last run and competed against nine rivals in that race, the LRPR would be:

LRPR = Starting Price LTO ÷ Runners LTO

LRPR = 5 ÷ 10 = 0.5

It is a simple matter to calculate this ratio for each runner which essentially is a guide to the degree of market confidence associated with the horse on its last run.

In order to put these figures in to context for a specific race, the value needs to be determined for every runner then a rank assigned to each in ascending order. Consequently the horse with the lowest LRPR figure would be ranked one, the next lowest two, and so on. These ranks can then be used in a forecasting model, or system, in the same way ability ratings are utilised. So a system may take the following form:

if LRPR Rank = 1

and .....

and .....

then bet

The first system I investigated using the LRPR was one applied to all weather handicaps and specifically the dual forecast bet. The analysis of the LRPR for these races showed an excellent correlation (see graph) and, given the dominance of the horses ranked 1 and 2, I thought there may be scope to exploit this Tote bet.

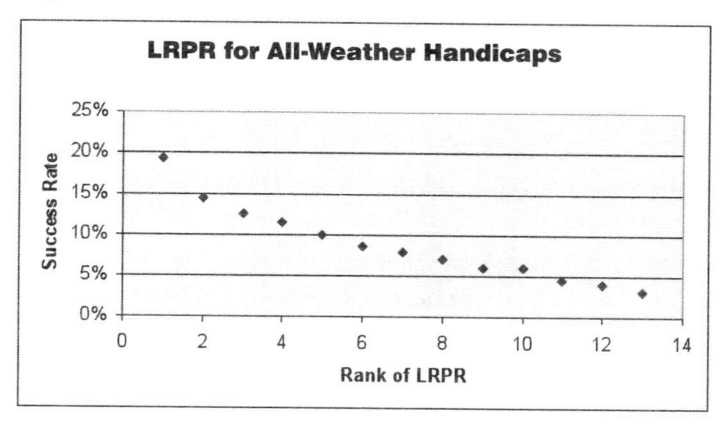

The dual forecast required the bettor to select the horses to finish first and second in either order; it has since been replaced by the Exacta which requires the horses to be selected in the correct order. Even though there is a huge over-round associated with the dual forecast, testing against the formbook produced good results so I immediately implemented the method during the winter of 1993/94.

Initial returns were good but I then ran into problems common to many systems. Firstly the win rate was exceptionally low at about 8%, less than one win in 12 bets.

Secondly the bet was not scalable. Even if the method made a good average profit, and I was able to keep betting during the prolonged losing spells, there was no way I could increase my return. The dual forecast was a pool bet and given the lack of liquidity at many meetings, increasing my stake would reduce the average profit and become self defeating.

The dual forecast was not a realistic option so I checked various other methods including focussing on horses for which the LRPR figure was less than specific thresholds, and the rank was in a certain range for different race grades, but could not find a profitable angle until I investigated novices' hurdle races, which was surprising because this race classification is a non-handicap.

The LRPR figure appeared to be a good starting point for developing systems for this race type and I soon had a method that appeared to have some potential. However on further analysis it was clear that the profitable horses were those which simply started at 2/1 or lower on their last run, so I was able to dispense with the calculation of the LRPR and modify the system accordingly. This can happen with system development. An initial idea is tested and refined then, from the analysis, a simpler solution is found which is more general and hence more reliable. The final system was given as:

> if novices' hurdle race and horse was beaten by no more than 10 lengths on last start and price for last start was 2/1 or lower then bet.

In 1996 I included this rule in my second book *Jump Racing For Profit* and the profit quoted for the years recorded was 13p/£ at industry starting price from 500 bets. Given the changes to this race category in recent years it is no surprise to see that the profit for this method has turned into a loss. However, it is interesting to note that in non-juvenile novices' hurdle races (ie those not restricted to three- or four-year-olds), the average profit to off time exchange prices for novices that started at 2/1 or lower on their last start and won that race, was 12p/£ from the last 1,400 bets. Easing the restrictions slightly so that the win can be in any of the runner's last three races makes the profit 9p/£ from approximately 2,000 bets.

In an attempt to widen my range of systems, during the winter of 1993/94 I started placing pool bets with the Tote, specifically the Placepot. The reason I did this was because I misguidedly thought I could make a long-term profit by using a selection system.

My approach was simple and used the information available in the *Racing Post*. I would select an all-weather meeting and place a star against the name of the horse which was top-rated by PostMark. In the event of joint top-rated runners I would use the one highlighted in the tipsters' selection box. I should add that this was before the *Racing Post* started to "adjust" their ratings, so a top-rated runner was the best horse on the figures, not one for which the ratings had been increased to make it top for a particular race. I starred the TopSpeed selections in a similar way and the Spotlight pick.

If I now had two or three different horses marked in the race I would move to the next contest. If all three stars were against the name of a single selection I would then look to the favourite in the forecast betting, and if that still gave me only one horse I would use the second favourite. This way I had at most three selections per race, and at least two. Therefore the fewest number of lines in my bet would be 64 and the most could be 729. However if there were more than 256 lines I would discard the meeting completely filing it under the "too random" category.

My theory, though flawed, was that using this expertise should give me an advantage in a pool bet where much of the money was placed on course by people looking for a fun bet and who would be making near random choices.

I was winning from time to time, then on 21 December 1993 the method found five winners and a placed runner in the six races on a day when three favourites failed to make the frame. The payout was 1447/1 and I was looking forward to collecting a decent amount the following day.

"I thought it was going to be you," the shop manager said in his usual brusque manner when I appeared at the counter with my winning ticket. "You'll have to wait until I've been to the bank."

While I waited I began to think about the Placepot, and I then realised how naive I had been placing these bets. I considered myself to be an astute bettor but I had fallen for the "win a fortune for a small stake" line. In fact I began to feel embarrassed that I had placed such poor value bets. At the time I could almost justify these bets by telling myself that any losses would benefit racing. However, since the sale of the Tote to BetFred, this is no longer the case and whereas the Tote's profits used to "stay in racing" now they "stay with BetFred". Eventually the manager returned and counted the money into an envelope for me; I paid it into my bank account immediately and ended my Placepot betting there and then.

On average a straight-win bet placed at industry starting price will return a long-term loss of about 23p/£. Modifying this to the race favourite reduces the loss to 7p/£. For the Placepot the loss is 27p/£, though high it is still better than other investment opportunities (see table).

Bet Type	Expected Loss
Win Bet All Favourites	-7p/£
Win Bet All Runners	-21p/£
Tote Placepot	-27p/£
Car or Domestic Appliance Warranties	-50p/£
National Lottery	-55p/£

The table illustrates the *value* of each investment in terms of expected long-term loss. Fortunately for win bets there is scope to reduce this figure, and in some cases turn it into a profit, by selecting the bets more carefully. However, this is not the case for the Placepot. For instance, you may sit down and go through the form in great detail eventually finding six long-priced horses, one in each race of a meeting, that you feel will make the frame. At the end of the afternoon you see that your hard work has paid off and your bet is a winner with each selection placed at prices of 25/1 or longer. But the payout is just 4/1, why? Well in each race a short-priced favourite also made the frame resulting in hundreds of winning tickets and a share barely worth collecting.

For the Placepot the potential profit is, to a large degree, out of the bettor's control. Essentially the return per line of the bet is random unless the six selections are all short-priced horses, in which case any positive return can be estimated but is likely to be very low. In other words, with a few exceptions, it is not possible to accurately predict the Placepot return for a group of six horses. Therefore over an extended period of time the loss to the bettor is likely to mirror the Tote take-out, 27p.

Amazingly this bet is preferable to some other investments such as the National Lottery or taking out a warranty for car repairs or domestic appliance cover. These gambles appeal in the same way as the Placepot: for a little cash you could get a huge return. However in the case of warranties the companies that promote them fail to point out that, although you may get lucky, or unlucky depending on your view, in the long term they will cost you a significant sum. At least with the National Lottery the slim chance of success is well known.

It still surprises me that when a new acquaintance finds out that I enjoy betting, the usual response is “that’s a mug’s game no-one wins at that”. Yet these are the same people who happily pay £50 per month to hedge against car repairs, or £10 a month for a warranty to cover a washing machine. Rather than taking out such poor-value investments they would be far better advised to put the monthly fee into a bank account. At least they would get back 102p/£, at today’s interest rates of two per cent, compared to just 50p/£ from the warranty provider.

Chapter Nine

The Price Is Everything

One issue that was raised on a regular basis while I was employed by the Potato Market Board was its closure. The threat was not from the potato growers who funded the organisation and benefited from its work, but from the British Government and European Union. Our own government, Conservative at the time, was ideologically opposed to organisations like the PMB whose actions prevented a totally free market. For instance, if a potato grower wanted to plant a larger acreage of potatoes then he or she had to either purchase quota from other growers, or pay an additional levy. In order to regulate production and avoid years of over and under supply, the area planted was controlled via a quota system, which necessitated these restrictions. The European Union also had problems with this and according to one government official, the fact that we were now "part of the United States of Europe meant that such controls should either be applied uniformly across all member states or be abolished".

How we survived for so long was a miracle and I lost count of the number of times the chief executive officer mentioned in meetings that he felt like he was "working under the sword of Damocles". I'm sure he read classics at university. Though the rest of the staff did not sense the cold metal edge of a sword suspended above their heads by a horse hair, they did fear the loss of employment. Consequently staff morale was rarely high especially during periods when the PMB was subject to parliamentary debate.

To lighten the atmosphere the statistics department's daily bet was introduced. We each made a selection and the bet, a patent, was put on by a member of the department at lunchtime. All winnings were retained and used to fund future bets and pay for tea and coffee. As far as the staff were concerned the daily bet was very successful; it is surprising how much a winning bet can lift spirits, and it was far more beneficial than any team-building exercise I had attended, and much cheaper.

During 1993 the threat of closure was beginning to concern me and the fact that I had finished studying for the MPhil meant that my work life was getting tedious. I also felt underemployed. The improved computer systems meant that I had very little to do and I was finding it extremely difficult to justify accepting a salary. While turning up at the office each morning was made bearable by my betting activities which at least provided an element of excitement during an otherwise totally predictable day, the office reorganisation that took place when the Board was closed between Christmas and New Year was the final straw as far as I was concerned.

When we returned on 2 January, 1994 the six offices on our floor had been merged into one, with the statistics department located in the centre of this newly formed open-plan office-space. The theory behind the change was that staff would hear others' conversations and would, as a result, improve their own knowledge of the workings of the PMB. In reality the only outcome of the redesign was to increase the overall level of noise within the room through more people chatting, telephones ringing, and filing cabinets opening and closing. Regarding an increase in knowledge sharing it, was now easier to shout across the room to a colleague to get the answer to a query, rather than looking it up or using any initiative. Although none of the staff approved of the changes the alterations were irreversible, open plan was the way forward. On that day I realised that my way forward was with a different company and started making plans to leave the PMB.

On 31 May, the day before the Erhaab's Derby, I left the Potato Marketing Board. My next job, with Raceform, did not start until 4 July so I had a month at home with Sara and our daughter, Rhianna, who had been born on 25 April (although I was at the hospital that evening I was not in the delivery suite opting instead to sit in the waiting room studying the formbook. It was Guineas week after all).

At the PMB I mainly took enquires relating to potato prices, yields and area planted; at Raceform the calls were mostly about Computer Raceform, the software package that essentially presented the formbook on the computer. Unlike today's excellent program, Raceform Interactive, the 1994 version was far from perfectly coded and was full of bugs. There were calls and queries to answer every day as users struggled with the program and, although constantly apologising for the frailties of the software was not a way I would choose to spend my time, the calls did bring me into contact with many interesting people, and most importantly a racing enthusiast named John.

Electronic data transfer was still quite rare, so the software was updated twice each week by floppy disk. These disks were wrapped in cardboard, enveloped and posted to all subscribers. Naturally there was a delay between posting and receipt of the data and John liked to keep up to date, so often he would call into the office to collect his disk. I had heard about professional punters, and had read Alex Bird's book, but when I first met John I could not believe I was shaking hands with a full-time professional bettor. Over a hundred questions flooded into my head, but I didn't launch into a protracted interview then. That could wait I thought.

Like Miles, John was tall and bearded but there the similarities stopped. John backed horses for a living, not for a distraction, and his bets were not in the three-figure range, they were four figures and up.

Over the years I got to know John very well, and he still uses my jumps ratings on a daily basis. His approach to betting was purely value-based and I was surprised to learn that it did not feature information from stables. It is easy to gain a false impression of these people especially if you read popular racing fiction. I thought that professional bettors, if they existed, would be connected to racing yards, trainers and jockeys, being fed inside information on which they would make their money. Nothing could have been further from the truth; John's success was down to hard work and good judgement.

The more time I spent talking to John the more I realised that he had an almost encyclopaedic knowledge of the sport. I was good at memorising results, and could visualise, and mentally replay, races which I had watched, but John went several steps further. If asked about any jumps horse John could give a detailed account of its form including likes and dislikes, and for particular races whether it had made any mistakes at fences or had been given a poor ride. So while a horse may be rated only modestly in a contest, John would adjust the figure if the animal had, uncharacteristically, not jumped particularly fluently through the race. Furthermore, he also retained information about the size of the horses, a fact which influenced his assessment markedly at certain tracks.

John's modus operandi was to assess each race at the meeting he was attending before leaving home. At the course he would arrive with a *Racing Post* on which he had written ratings against the names of the runners. One set was Timeform figures, and I believe the other source was Superform. Comments were also written against some animals' names, and above the forecast odds he would write his own tissue (his opinion of the value price for each runner).

Before the race he would inspect the horses in the pre-parade ring and then again in the main ring. Interestingly he would make sure he saw every horse in the race, and that included those with only a remote chance of success. Depending on what he saw he would make further notes, which he would transcribe into his computer after racing, and adjust his tissue slightly. Moving to the course he would then repeat this process as the runners moved to post. Only then would he consider betting. All bets were placed on course and he would only bet if he could beat his tissue. This was his main rule, one which he never even considered breaking.

On one occasion he was preparing to go to Ascot when he telephoned the office. We had a chat and I said that I thought a runner in the handicap chase was worth a bet. He agreed saying that it was the most likely winner and he would back it at 15/8. The horse in question opened at 13/8, was cut to 6/4, so I backed it; the price was then cut again and the horse eventually started at 11/10. Seeing the price moves and knowing John's views, I thought he was on so I telephoned him that evening. Not only had John ignored the horse, he had backed an alternative runner in the race. I was surprised but as he explained the horse was not offered at 15/8 or better so he considered it to be poor value. Such strict application of rules is essential for value bettors and system players alike.

Developing an odds line, or price tissue, is an attractive solution to the horseracing problem. With exchanges betting to an over-round of just one per cent, it is natural to assume that, by adding a little *personal expertise*, it should be possible to translate that minimal in-built loss into a profit. But as with so many aspects of betting what appears to be simple in theory is extremely complex in practice.

One of the problems associated with the creation of an accurate tissue is its evaluation. This may at first seem to be a trivial obstacle to overcome, after all if the proportion of winners reflects the tissue price then the odds line should be accurate. Unfortunately while that may be the case, it does not necessarily result in a profit. For example, the results of a simplistic odds line are given in the following table.

ANALYSIS OF ODDS LINE RESULTS

Odds Line	Number of Observations	Expected Number of Winners	Actual Number of Winners
2/1	183	61	60
3/1	836	209	209
4/1	2125	425	425
5/1	3942	657	657
6/1	5173	739	740
7/1	6104	763	766
8/1	6984	776	778
9/1	7329	732	736
10/1	7744	704	705
11/1	7452	621	623
12/1	5694	438	439
13/1	3682	263	263

Odds Line	Number of Observations	Expected Number of Winners	Actual Number of Winners
14/1	2025	135	135
15/1	1568	98	98
16/1	935	55	57
17/1	522	29	29
18/1	456	24	24
19/1	480	24	24
20/1	147	7	7
Total	**63381**	**6760**	**6775**

A price was determined for each of the 63,381 runners in the test data set. These prices are shown in the table together with the expected number of winners for each price. Horses rated as 2/1 on the odds line should win at a rate of one in three approximately. Therefore for the 183 horses in this group there should have been 61 winners. The *Actual Number of Winners* column shows how many horses associated with each price won. In theory this figure should match the expected number of winners if the odds line is accurate. From the table it can be seen that, in the main, there is a high degree of agreement between these two sets of figures which illustrates that the runners are winning at the expected rate and the tissue can be considered accurate with respect to the win ratio.

The odds-line theory states that once an accurate tissue has been created, making a profit is simply a matter of backing those runners for which the price available is greater than the tissue price indicates it should be. In other words, if the tissue is an accurate measure of the chance of success then beating this price should result in a profit. Using the test data, and following this rule, would have returned a loss of 31p/£ at industry starting price. In fact a better option was to back all runners which had a starting price lower than the tissue price, these lost just 11p/£. So what has gone wrong?

Within each price band there is a distribution of horses with a variety of starting prices. The figures used to evaluate the tissue are based on all of the runners and it is fair to assume that the shorter priced runners will inflate the ratio making it appear accurate. Therefore the test that was applied to determine the accuracy of the odds line was not valid. Simply having a tissue which accurately classifies the runners by price does not guarantee a profit. By applying the odds-line rule regarding the price comparison we have sub divided the data into two sets: in one set we have the horses which did not meet the price threshold, and in the other we have those which did. So the test of accuracy should be, "Does the tissue accurately reflect the number of winners which are priced longer than the odds line?" The group which does not pass the price test should be ignored and not form part of the evaluation process.

I have read similarly flawed arguments applied to the *Racing Post* betting forecast. Although the number of winners associated with each price given in this forecast is in line with the expected number based on the prices themselves, simply backing all runners which are priced longer than the forecast will not return a profit in the long term.

In the past I have found that in order to make an automated odds line profitable it is necessary to introduce a price element into calculation. Consequently the tissue should be made up of the relevant horse and trainer data, plus the current price available. Furthermore price movements over a fixed period of time are also useful inputs, as well as other significant data which is often overlooked.

Without stable information it is difficult to believe that John's tissue price would be better than that produced by the bookmakers, after all he had the same data on which to base his assessment. John's advantage was two-fold: he could accurately reduce race results, trainer statistics, and other formbook information into a single price; he could then precisely adjust this by his observations in the paddock and of the horses on the way to post. This seemingly minimal edge was converted into a significant profit year after year. He is simply the best judge of a racehorse I know.

John was not the only professional punter who used Computer Raceform. Another I came to know fairly well was Tony. He did more closely fit the stereotype having contacts in many of the main racing yards and a very large personality to match his very large physique. While he was clearly an expert of horserace assessment, and someone who did well from the sport, I would favour John's views over his.

So within a few months I had gained a new set of racing colleagues who were not just enthusiastic amateurs but serious professionals for whom the racecourse was a place of work. Up to that point I was not totally convinced that such people really existed. Yet, on the day Master Oats won the Welsh National at Newbury we were stood around the pre-parade ring and I was talking to one professional punter about a front-running non-trier he had recently spotted, and another was cradling Rhianna in his arms trying to get her to sleep, while explaining to Sara that with the money he had lost since Boxing Day he could have purchased a new house.

Racecourse conversations had now moved on. No longer were there references to how a horse may have worked at home, or that a stable was feeling confident about a particular runner. A detailed knowledge of the formbook was assumed so, for instance, stating that a horse which finished second to a runner in the race we were examining had since won, was not adding to the overall pool of information. Instead the discussion concerned interpreting the results and drawing inferences from them. For example, would a horse that had run his best races at tracks like Newton Abbot and Stratford be suited by a big open course like Newbury? Did this horse behave previously in the parade ring in the same manner it did today? Does a runner's action on the way to post suggest that he will be suited by the prevailing going?

Formbook results were available to all, bettors and layers alike, so in order to gain an advantage it was necessary to use these results in a more sophisticated way and to include other data, such as that gained from the parade ring, in order to *add value* to the analysis. John was capable of making connections and drawing inferences I would never have considered; in terms of our Shakespearean analogy he could not only quote every line from every play, but also give a detailed meaning of each plot twist and theme.

The ultimate aim of this knowledge acquisition and analysis was a value price for each runner. Once this was established John would apply his system: if he could beat the price then he would back the horse. Importantly he was not trying to determine which horse would win a race, but the chance of each horse winning. I appreciate that this approach to value betting does not sit comfortably with some bettors. Many prefer to adopt a method that is based on finding winners which is due possibly to the complexity of the value concept.

The idea of a value bet is not easy to fully understand. Often a racing commentator will state that he is opting for a longer priced runner "to find some value". It is remarks of this nature that cloud the argument and lead to a degree of misunderstanding by bettors trying to follow a value-betting strategy. A runner is not value simply because it is offered at a long price. As an example, if I raced against Usain Bolt over 50 metres (I always struggled to get the full 100-metre trip) then taking the 33/1 about me winning would not be value (unless you happened to know that a trip wire was placed in

Bolt's lane). Even though the return from the 1/999 offered about Bolt would be meagre, I can assure you it would be excellent value.

While discussing the value problem with a probability lecturer at the university he produced a 10p coin, flipped and caught it and asked me to estimate the chance that it had landed on heads. I replied that it was 0.5 since there were two equal outcomes. His reply surprised me, "But the event is over," he said, "so surely it is either one or zero?"

This is the view the winner-finding group take. There must be only one value bet in each race since, ignoring dead-heats, there can only be one winner. Therefore if you find the winner you have found the value. In other words, if your horse that started at 10/1 and should have been 5/1 loses, it can then be viewed as a poor-value bet since no odds can compensate for failure.

This argument has some merit, but only applies after the race has been run. Before the contest starts the 10/1 shot was a value bet. It is the result of the race that changes the view of the event and the meaning of a value price. While the horses are at the start there can be several value bets because each horse has a chance of success which may be understated by the price on offer. Given paradoxes of this nature it is no surprise that punters can fall into either the winner-finding group or be classified as value hunters with both factions seeing the logic of their respective approaches.

To illustrate the concept of value the example of coin

flipping is often used, and it is usually stated that getting 11/10 about heads would be good value, whereas getting 4/5 about tails would be an example of poor value. That is true, but it is not directly comparable to horseracing. For coin flipping the chance of success is known to a small degree of tolerance, providing the coin is unbiased, and the event can be repeated.

For horseracing the chance of success for each runner in unknown and the event cannot be repeated. The same runners may line up on several occasions but the exact race can never be repeated. Although this sounds ominous for punters hoping to make a profit, it is in fact to the bettors' advantage. If the exact chance of success was known for all runners it would be a simple matter for bookmakers to compile a set of prices which guaranteed them a positive return and made it impossible for the bettor to win. This is why casino games such as roulette offer no possible chance of a long-term profit to players.

A more appropriate example would be if someone held a bag of coins, each with varying biases, and took each coin individually and flipped it offering a price about heads or tails. After watching many trials you may establish that, in general, the biases suggest 4/6 about heads is a fair price. And when the person flips the coin from a starting position of heads facing upwards, this price offers excellent value. So if offered 4/5 under these circumstances about heads you would bet with confidence. Essentially you have reduced the event to an abstraction of key factors then applied a method which highlights the value bets. In retrospect, on a flip-by-flip basis this method will have found some value bets (winners) and other bets (losers) but it should be profitable and hence considered to be a winning value-based approach. Notice also that this solution takes the form of a betting system.

Obviously applying this approach to horseracing is much more difficult than coin flipping. The number of variables involved makes the task more complex and the fact that each race features horses competing against each other further complicates the matter. This is where systems can be most useful.

A profitable betting system is value betting in the purest sense. John would ask me why I would back a horse simply because it qualified under one of my rules yet the price offered no value. I would explain that the system partitioned the domain and was applied to only a small number of variables. Based on these data the selections were value in the long-term, even though some individual selections were not if alternative measures of value were used.

There is an obvious conflict though. In many systems a qualifier would be considered a bet regardless of the price, unless the price formed part of the rule. And this can lead to difficulties. If the system, or variants of it, become widely known then the selections will become over-bet resulting in the method failing. Again this could be categorised as an unwanted external influence but it is something that should be constantly monitored.

One way to do this is to keep a check of the win rate and profit. If the expected number of winners is maintained but the profit starts to decline, then it suggests that the method has been unearthed and the prices available have been adjusted accordingly. This was the problem with the original novices' chase system. One way to make such a system last a little longer is to start backing the selections early in the day. Although this will not always solve the problem, in some cases it will extend the life of the method and is worth considering.

While I was working for Raceform Miles and Gill were parting company and we met them on very few occasions that year. Of course having a baby in our house also contributed to this reduction in socialising. However, Miles and I did go to Bath to back Roger Charlton's Splinter. Though not thought of in the same terms as Magic Of Life, Splinter was considered to be a useful two-year-old. The colt was due to make his debut in the last race of the afternoon and we arrived just before the conditions stakes opting to miss the first three races which were just run-of-the-mill handicaps. Miles gave the member of staff on the gate a fiver and he let us both in. Splinter opened very short, much shorter than we had hoped, but he comfortably beat his eight rivals and we returned home in profit. That was the only time I ever went racing at Bath and the last time I went racing with Miles.

Chapter Ten

Will it Still Work Tomorrow?

My time as an employee at Raceform was short-lived, during which time I was suffering from a thyroid condition which meant I lost 21lbs in six weeks, was permanently exhausted, and had uncontrollable bouts of shaking. By the autumn of 1995 I was back at Oxford Brookes University. I had been offered a place, with a small bursary, to read for a PhD and to teach for up to six hours a week. This was an opportunity I felt I could not turn down. Admittedly the money was not on a par with my previous salary, but the chance to continue researching artificial intelligence more than made up for the loss of income.

The single critical factor which made this move possible was Sara's support. I could not have switched to a job paying less than £10,000 per year without it; like so many areas of life it is near impossible to do the things you really want to do without the help, guidance and assurance of someone you can count on to always back you. This is especially true when confronted by family and friends who struggle to accept an unconventional lifestyle. The question I get asked more than any other is: "When are you going to get a real job?" Having someone in your corner makes these awkward discussions easier to handle.

The PhD course was full-time so I was assigned two

university supervisors, Dr Nigel Crook and Dr Nic Wilson. Both are experts in artificial intelligence. For the MPhil I chose expert systems for the main focus of my study, but this time I opted for connectionist systems, specifically identifying methods for generating explanations from artificial neural networks.

As researchers have become more aware of the structure and processing methods of the brain, the temptation to replicate it on a machine has become overwhelming. Artificial neural networks have been inspired by the limited knowledge gained from these biological advances.

Like the brain, artificial neural networks consist of many connected neurons (nodes), although the number differs significantly between the two mechanisms. It has been suggested that the human brain has approximately 10^{11} active nodes on average, whereas the number in its artificial equivalent will rarely exceed a few thousand.

The biological neurons receive many signals which are modified by a biochemical weight at the receiving synapse. These weighted inputs are combined by the soma (or body cell) and under appropriate circumstances the neuron transmits a signal.

The mechanics of artificial nodes are modelled on these processes, where incoming signals are adjusted by weights, are summed and, dependent on the activation function, a strong or weak signal is passed to the connecting nodes. Although similarities exist between biological and artificial neural networks, they differ in both function and form, especially how the nodes are connected and pass signals. The artificial network is, as one would expect, very much a simplification of the biological network.

Essentially, neural networks learn by example. Unlike expert systems they need no formal programming nor any initial coding of knowledge relating to the problem under consideration. Instead, the network formulates its own knowledge from the examples it encounters during a period of training. Although this approach may seem somewhat ad hoc, it has been shown that neural networks can identify relationships between the data which had previously been overlooked by experienced domain experts. In fact, it has been proved that given a sufficient number of hidden nodes, a neural network can be trained to perform any mapping operation. It is, therefore, easy to see the appeal of these networks given their simplicity of construction and classification power.

For a specific class of neural networks the output is a value between zero and one in the form of a probability. For example, if a network of this type was trained to classify movements in the stock market where a closing price above an opening price was indicated by a "1" in the system and the reverse a "0", then an output of 0.8 would suggest that there was an 80% chance of the day producing an increase in the value of the stock.

The appeal of these methods to someone interested in

horseracing is obvious. Representing winners with a "1" and losers with a "0" produces a system which will estimate the chance of success for each runner in the race.

Neural networks are, in principle, capable of solving any non-linear classification problem which illustrates the degree of flexibility associated with these systems. Although statistical techniques have been used with high levels of success for many forecasting problems, these methods are often very data dependent, with noisy or missing data leading to erroneous conclusions. Neural networks, on the other hand, are much more tolerant under these conditions and it has been reported that these systems often outperform symbolic approaches when the domain information is incomplete or contains noisy data. In my view, neural networks are the perfect computer-based modelling tool for racing enthusiasts.

Creating a neural network is much the same as generating a betting system. There are four distinct steps: data processing, design of the network architecture, network training/testing and, finally, validation. For a horseracing network the data processing phase concerns deciding which components will be used to form the model and how they are represented. Such items could include weight carried, previous race performance variables, trainer data, days off the track, among others, and could be used with or without pre-processing. So the previous race finishing position may be capped at ten, or represented as a percentage of the number of runners in the race with a horse finishing last represented as 0%, and the winner 100%. The weight a horse carries, though, may be used without any modification, so 9-00 would be input as 126.

Other forms of data representation can also be adopted. The LRPR figure, for example, could be included rather than the previous race starting price. However, using the starting price and number of runners from the previous race individually may result in the network making its own more appropriate connection between these two variables and the runner's chance of success.

It has been argued that numerical representations of qualitative physical properties are invalid since they are merely an abstraction, and this is why neural networks will always be destined to fall below an acceptable level of performance. This is nonsense, of course. Humans also represent concepts in abstract form and that does not cloud their meaning nor invalidate the processing methods. For instance, we may detect that something is hot without having to convert it to a numerical form. The network could process this as a single input with "1" indicating hot, and "0" representing not hot, alternatively it could use the actual temperature. Both instances use numbers rather than concepts but both are valid.

A horseracing example may concern the attributes of a particular runner. The horse may be described as "better on soft ground" which is easily understood and processed by an experienced racing enthusiast. However it is imprecise in its form. How much better is the horse on this type of ground? And how soft does the going have to be before the horse runs to its best? Even a racing expert may find it difficult to provide satisfactory answers to these queries. In fact the only way to accurately answer these questions to an acceptable degree of precision is to use an alternative scale to represent the concept and, although abstract, what better scale is there than numbers? Both humans and computers use this transformation to process complex concepts in many areas of life, not just horseracing.

The second step in neural network development concerns its architecture. This may include fixing the number of inputs, or if the network has more than one layer, deciding on the number of hidden nodes as well as identifying the class of network to use, and the learning method. The complexity of the network depends on the domain on which it is required to generate the forecasts. A simple domain will only require a few hidden nodes otherwise it could produce a model that has been over trained. In these cases the network very accurately represents the training data but in most instances does not generalise well to a new set of data. A parallel with a system would be one that has resulted from a data-mining exercise and has been made too specific. Although these models and systems have good historical performance, they fail when presented with new cases.

Network training is an iterative process: networks are

trained, tested and either retained or discarded. There are different ways to determine when training should be suspended such as using the mean squared error or by using a separate test set of data. Naturally the speed of training is dependent on the number of training patterns available. As the number of training patterns increases the time it takes to train the network also increases. However, it is necessary to ensure the training data adequately represents the domain the network is trying to emulate, so a sufficient number of training records is required. Although these models are able to perform well in sparsely populated domains, better coverage will produce a better model.

Finally the model needs to be validated against a completely new set of data before it is implemented. A similar process can be used for system creation. An initial concept is validated with respect to its applicability and efficacy, and the data organised into a form that allows this idea to be investigated in detail. The structure of the system then needs to be set. For horseracing systems this could mean deciding between an "on the day" approach which highlights qualifiers each day based purely on historical results, or a "horses to follow" method which creates a list of runners to back in the future. The rule, or system, can then be checked against historical data and modified if required. Once a satisfactory set of results has been achieved the rule can be validated. Though often thought less important, this final step of validating the method is the most critical.

On completion of a new system the question on every system developer's mind, and the question I get asked most often, is: How can I tell if the system will work in the future? This is a difficult problem to resolve and is compounded by the fact that after developing a method we desperately want it to work. After all we have invested time and effort in creating the rule and if it fails then that time has been wasted. Furthermore it means that our initial idea may have been flawed. Consequently a plus sign against the average profit for the test data is a welcome sight and one that is readily accepted, in many cases too readily accepted as a guide to future profits.

While validation of a method is critical, whether a system is profitable after implementation is a result of the complete system development process. Was the initial idea valid? Are there a sufficient number of cases to form the rule? Is the profit significantly higher than zero? Has the validation process been followed correctly? If you can answer "yes" to these questions then your system has a reasonable chance of making a profit in the future. However a profit is still not guaranteed. Consider the following for example:

ANALYSIS OF THE TAA3 SYSTEM

Year	Wins	Runs	Wins%	Profit*/£
2005	61	501	12.2%	0.35
2006	77	559	13.8%	0.16
2007	85	501	17.0%	0.21
2008	61	433	14.1%	0.17
2009	98	593	16.5%	0.21
All Runners	382	2587	14.8%	0.22

* profit given to exchange prices recorded at off time

Spanning five years the system detailed above found 2,587 qualifiers of which 382 won producing a profit of 22p/£. Based on these findings the initial idea seems to be valid; the size of the sample seems reasonable, the average profit is certainly higher than zero and the method was validated rigorously. Obviously this is a method that should make a profit. However in 2010 it found 105 winners from 706 bets and returned a loss of 11p/£, illustrating the fact that future profits can never be guaranteed.

Fortunately this example is extreme and, although it is not possible to be certain about the future of any system, it is possible to eliminate many that are destined to fail by applying a range of validation techniques and checks.

In order to undertake a completely unbiased evaluation of the system, it is necessary to divide the initial pool of data into three partitions. Many developers assume that only two sets are needed: one for developing and refining the system and a second for testing. Often this division takes the form of even-numbered years or race numbers for system development and the remainder for testing. However this is not adequate simply due to the iterative process of the development phase. A system which produces good results from the development data is checked against the test data. If the results are not as good as expected the original model is refined and the process is repeated.

Once the results for both sets are found to be satisfactory then the method is assumed to be reliable. However, even though two data sets have been used, the process itself has resulted in a system that has been optimised on both sets rather than just the development data. Therefore it is bound to produce good results. This is why a third data set is required. Once the system development and testing process have been completed, the method should be validated against this new data set, data which has not formed any part of the system creation process. If the results for this new set are in line with previous findings, then the method has a better chance of succeeding.

The following example illustrates the importance of the validation data. Development and test data indicated that this high-volume method would return a profit of just over 9p/£ at racetime exchange prices before commission. The longest priced winner was just 28/1 and, when taken with the huge sample size, over 20,000 bets, it gave the system a solid look. The graph of these results only serves to reinforce this view.

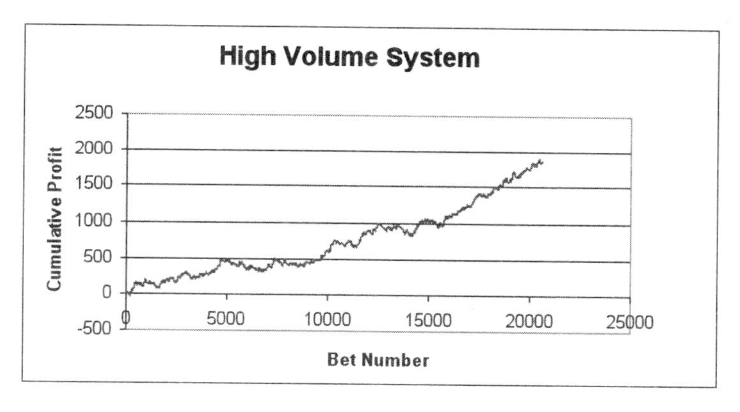

In graphical form the system has the perfect arrangement, a steadily increasing line demonstrating how the total profit from the method kept improving without too many erratic periods causing the figure to drop. Based on this graph alone a system player could be forgiven for jumping in and betting immediately, before even performing any form of validation. However, the 3,000-case validation set, which covered a period starting at the end of the test data, made just 81 points profit which equated to just under 3p/£ before commission and resulting in a probable loss (see next graph on page 184). This type of degradation is common with systems: the "new" data rarely matches the historical returns simply due to the optimisation applied to the development and test data even when the sample size is large.

Unfortunately even if the validation set produces good results, the system could still fail if there is a high degree of variability in the profit and loss figures. The following graph

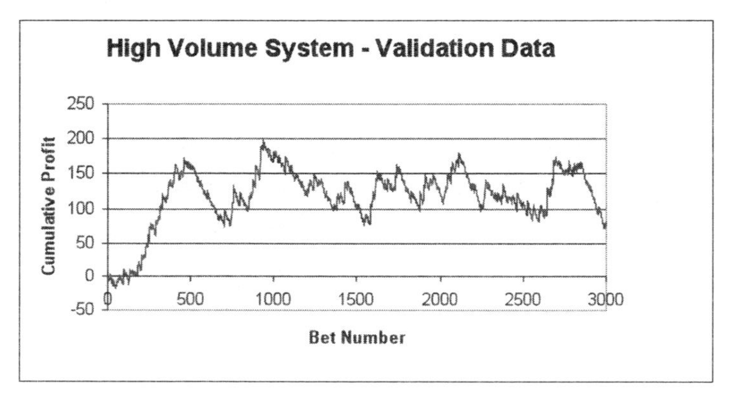

shows the cumulative return from a system possessing a high degree of variability. The long losing runs are apparent. Note the period between bet 1,000 and bet 2,000, with large increases representing long-priced winners. Such systems are difficult to validate accurately. The next 1,300 bets highlighted by this system, for example, made a loss of 305 points, equivalent to an average loss of 23p/£.

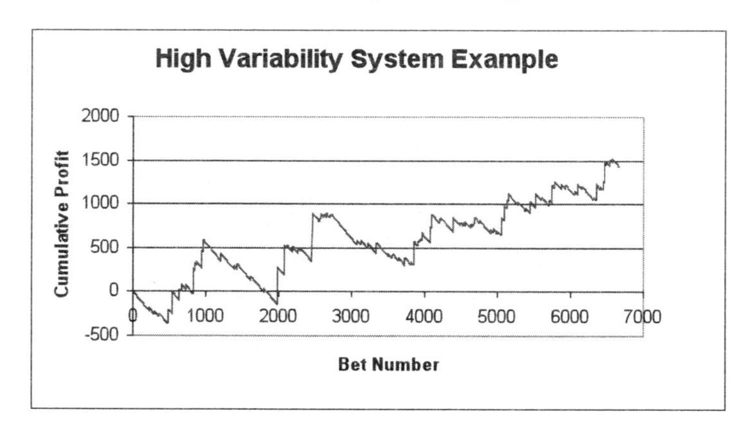

There are mathematical techniques, such as confidence intervals and those based on chi squared tests that can be applied which provide a guide to the level of future profits. These determine a numerical estimate of the chance the approach has of succeeding and take into account the variability of the data and the sample size. But it is important to remember that these tests will only produce meaningful results if they are applied to the validation data alone. Again if these validation statistics are based on the complete data set, they are almost certain to indicate the system is sound when in actual fact it may not be.

As an alternative, less mathematical method for dealing with systems presenting high degrees of variability, the validation data should be sorted into an order based on the return from each bet. There will be many return figures which are -1 indicating losers, but there should also be several positive returns.

From these figures calculate how many positive returns the total profit is based on. This is easily performed on a spreadsheet but, if you do not have access to one, a calculator is just as good. Enter the total return from the results, then subtract the profit from the longest priced winner. If the total is still above zero, repeat with the next highest value. Continue until the profit has been reduced to zero. If it takes only a few bets to eliminate the profit then it is likely that there is a high degree of variation in the validation set with respect to profit, and that the number of observations is too low, so any conclusions are likely to be unreliable. In this instance either more independent data needs to be found, or the system should be run to zero stakes until a satisfactory sample size is reached.

This final check is especially important when using exchange price data. There may well be a very long-priced winner, such as 200.0 or higher, which can inflate the overall average profit, but is unlikely to be repeated when the method is implemented. For the previous High Variability system the profit from the 6,664 bets relied on just four winners. Without those the system would be in overall deficit.

The validation process provides a great deal of information, not just a summary of figures which can be tested to see if they are in keeping with expectations. As well as providing an invaluable test on new data, it can be used to check for other influencing factors. As an example consider the following two systems. Both are based on all-weather racing and target a similar weakness in the exchange market. They were developed and tested on data taken from 2005 to 2010 with the 2011 calendar year used as the validation set. Both methods returned a profit from 2011 as follows (all figures are given before commission):

ANALYSIS OF TWO SYSTEMS

System	Wins	Runs	Wins%	Profit*/£
A	254	858	30%	0.08
B	124	413	30%	0.18

* profit given to exchange prices recorded at off time

Fortunately both methods made a healthy profit. System A had over twice as many bets as System B and returned a total profit of 70.08 points to a level 1 point stake. Though System B had fewer bets the average profit at 18 per cent was much higher and in total it made just over five points more than System A. Interestingly they both had a 30 per cent win rate, but which one should be implemented?

System B is more attractive given the much higher profit figure and it is tempting to implement it without further investigation but plotting the results by bet number casts a different light on the systems' merits.

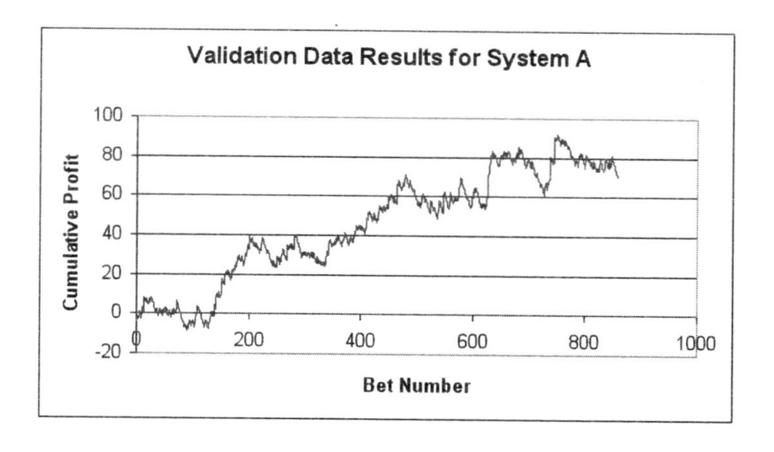

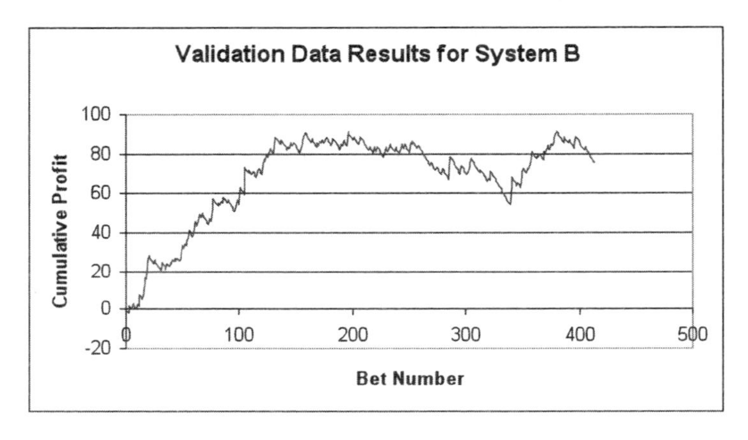

The bulk of the profit for System B came in the early months of the year. The method then flatlined for the remainder of the validation period. Given such a graph it is tempting to structure a staking plan to maximise the return for this seasonal pattern. But making adjustments to the system itself, or the staking plan, at such a late stage of system development is always a dangerous option. Theoretically, if changes are made then these need to be validated on another set of data, and in this case one is not available. For these systems I maintained a level stake for both throughout 2012, but with one point per bet on System B and four points per bet on System A, simply due to the gradually increasing return this system exhibited and the fact that System B had not made a profit for over 200 bets.

To provide a statistical check on the validation data the z-test can be used. This test verifies whether or not two means are drawn from the same population. For a systems based on data mining the development data can be biased, hence the requirement for the validation process. Once applied, the z-test will indicate whether or not the mean of the validation data is in line with the mean from the development data taking into account the sample sizes and variability. Its calculation is relatively straightforward, requiring the user to determine arithmetic means and standard deviations for the development and validation data, before applying the test. Alternatively the standard z-test function available in excel can be employed. As an example consider the following graph which presents the development and validation data for a system I was testing in 2012. The vertical line separates the two data sets.

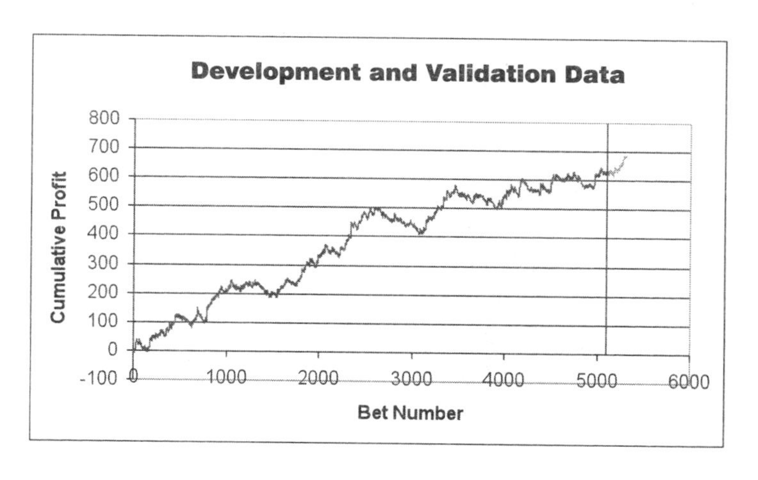

The system had made 630 points profit from just over 5,000 bets; an average profit of just over 12%. Based on these data the system clearly warranted further testing. The first 200 bets during the validation test produced a 57 point profit, an average profit of 28%. At this stage the system looked like a viable option. However the z-test suggested that the two means (12% and 28%) were significantly different. The reason for this is that the test can be applied in a two-tailed form which tests whether the two means are different, rather than a one-tailed test which simply ascertains whether one mean is lower or higher than the other.

For horseracing systems it is easy not be too concerned if the validation data out performs the development data, after all the system has continued to make a profit. But is such a result reliable? Why should the validation data produce much higher returns than the development data? In fact, the opposite would be expected due to the optimisation applied to the development cases.

This is one of the benefits of the two-tailed z-test, in these cases it acts as a warning that the validation data may not be accurately reflecting the potential of the system and that more data should be collected before implementation. The following graph shows the profit from the extended validation set which reached almost 1,000 cases.

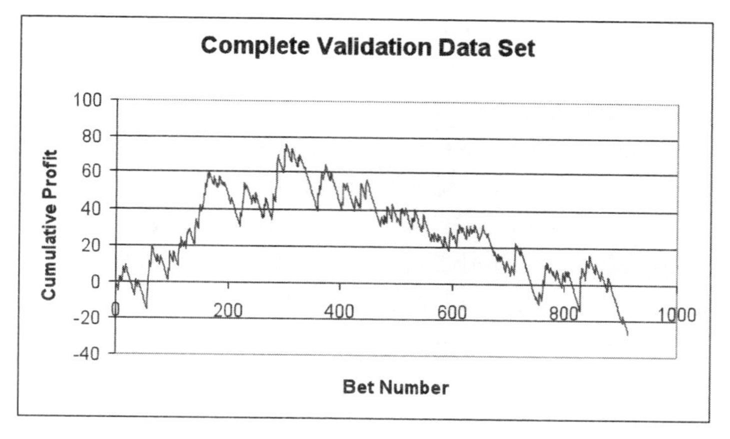

Again the z-test suggests that the two means are significantly different, but this time the validation data average is far lower than would be expected since it had dropped to -3%. Had I implemented the system at an earlier stage without checking the z-statistic it would have been very costly.

Seasonal variations are common in systems and it is easy to over-react to them. For instance a method may produce a consistent profit through the year except for September and October. Should these months be omitted? If so, this means that a horse may be a qualifier on 31 August, yet if the meeting is cancelled and the runner declared to race a day later, it would not be a qualifier. Unless there is a good reason, then a calendar date should not have such a profound influence on the performance of a system.

Obviously there is one key date in the year, namely 1st January, when the age of the runners increases, which can be important, but other months are not so significant. Normally in these cases it is not the date that is causing the problem but some other variable which is not uniformly distributed over time and therefore has more impact in certain months. To illustrate how this can negatively affect the performance of a model consider the following case study which was recorded when neural networks were a relatively new classification tool.

The defence department of a large western state wanted a system that could identify, from a visual feed, its own tanks from those of potentially hostile forces. A neural network was suggested and it was decided to test its applicability on photographic evidence before constructing a more complete system. Images were taken of tanks from various countries and fed into the network.

Once the system was fully trained it was tested and found to exhibit a 100 per cent success rate. It seemed too good to be true, and it was. When it was used in the field the success rate was far lower, in fact it hardly categorised any of the tanks correctly. At first the staff were perplexed and confused. How could a computer system that had performed so well during initial testing fail so badly once tested outside the laboratory? The answer was, as it normally is, in the data. Images for the home nation's tanks had been created on a day when the sky was blue and there was no sign of rain. However for the other tanks the photographs were taken on a cloudy day. The network could easily discriminate between the two sets of images, not by the shape of the tank but by the cloudiness of the sky.

For our horseracing example with the two poor autumn months, the reason the system underperforms at this point will not be due simply to the time of year. It is more likely to be an alternative influencing variable such as a higher degree of long course absences by the qualifiers. Many National Hunt runners have a break over the summer and return to racing in the autumn and this bias may have a negative impact on the performance of the method. If this were the case then the time of year is not the key factor, it is more to do with the issue of fitness for horses returning after a break. This would impact on all months but is only apparent from the time analysis for the period when their number is significant. In this instance an analysis by days off the track should provide the figures required in order to make the correct judgement.

If the system has passed all of the tests and there is nothing in the validation results to suggest any unwanted biases, then it has a good chance of succeeding. However, being cautious, I would still run it to low stakes for a period of time in order to ensure that the correct qualifiers are found, whether it is possible to implement the method accurately, and to identify if there are any hidden factors not apparent from the testing which could turn the expected profit into a loss.

In the TAA3 example given earlier, the 2010 returns were exceptionally poor even though the system had been checked and validated thoroughly. There is a hint in the results why this happened. For the historical years the highest number of qualifiers was 598 but in 2010 this figure jumped to 706. After checking I found no new external factors which could explain why the performance of the model had changed, which is the usual case, so merely put it down to a freak year.

In 2011 I ran the method again and the results were more in line with expectations with 98 winners from 613 bets and a profit of 17p/£. Essentially one poor year does not invalidate a method which is based on sound principles and has been developed correctly. Admittedly it is off-putting, but under these circumstances do not abandon the approach entirely, at the very least continue to run it either with very low stakes or a zero stake. If it was a statistical blip then the profit will return along with your betting confidence and you can then exploit the method to its full potential.

Keeping faith in a new system can depend very much on the staking plan used. While the validation process may suggest the system will work, a poor early run combined with a high stake can easily cast doubts in the system player's mind. This is exactly what happened to me in 1990 with the novice chasers' method. In that instance I was correct to assume the system was no longer worth following, but since then I have aborted systems under similar circumstances which later proved to be profitable. This is precisely why I stake a new system very low; the theoretical results may be convincing but it is the return from a live-test phase which provides the necessary level of confidence.

Even after a satisfactory initial live trial, some systems can be difficult to follow simply due to the long losing runs. Again adopting a sensible staking plan and setting the stake at a reasonable level can help with this. There are almost as many staking plans as there are systems and, while many of the more complex approaches suggest they can improve the overall return, it is important to remember that these methods are optimised on the historical results of the system to which they are applied.

If the future results differ from those on which the method has been built, then the staking plan will not necessarily improve the level of profit and can in some cases turn a winning method into a losing one. Having a system which produced a profit that mirrored the historical average return but cost money due to the staking plan is very difficult to accept. This is why I tend to opt for a level stakes plan or, very occasionally, a cover-to-win approach where the stake is determined by the price with the aim of winning a fixed amount per bet.

If a system forms part of a portfolio of methods, then the stakes between the approaches can be varied, but kept constant for each individual method. So a one point-per-bet stake may be applied to System A, but this could be increased to five points per bet for System B and so on. The most obvious way to set the level of stake for each system is to relate it directly to the expected profit. So the largest stake would be placed on the system with the highest historical profit.

This, in theory at least, should guarantee the maximum profit, providing the methods continue to perform in line with expectations. But consider these results for a system I used until recently: for a six-year time period the method found 9,886 bets and made a profit of 12p/£ (£11,380 to a level £10 stake). Given the good rate of return and the seemingly high degree of reliability indicated by the large number of bets, this method could attract a higher-than-average number of points per bet than other systems in the portfolio. However, this method had two key disadvantages. Firstly the win rate was just 2%; and secondly the longest losing run was 373. Having the largest stake on the most profitable system is logical, but if the system has the similar characteristics to this one then it would become very difficult to follow.

Therefore, the approach I have adopted over the years is to base the stake on the win rate, not the profit margin. So a system such as the one just detailed would in all probability have the lowest stake per bet, and one boasting a good success rate of, say, 30% would have the highest. This may not maximise the profit of the portfolio but, with the bigger bets winning more often, the temptation to amend the methods or drop some systems at an early stage is reduced. Psychologically this is an easier strategy to follow and maintain.

Naturally I created many neural networks during the research for the PhD, some of which were based on horseracing. But the aim of the research was to extract rules and generate explanations from the networks, so essentially they acted merely as a vehicle to test other techniques. Fortunately the research did show that networks could be trained, then decompiled so that the relationships found between the variables were more visible. This has applications for horseracing bettors who wish to determine more obscure rules for use as betting systems, and anyone who has an interest in neural networks should consider including a rule-extraction method solely for this purpose. Betting systems based on these rules are less likely to be found by others and as a result will have a longer life.

Unlike an MPhil, a PhD is more theoretical, and consequently I spent a considerable proportion of my time in libraries, both at the university and at the Bodleian in Oxford. When I first joined the Bodleian Library in the early 1980s, I was required to sign a declaration in front of an important official who witnessed the solemn words I was forced to utter. In this cathedral-like edifice, it almost seemed a religious rite that I had to perform.

Firstly, I promised faithfully that I would not, under any circumstances, remove or damage any of the precious tomes that packed the dusty shelves towering in every direction. Imagine my surprise when my pledge was extended still further. Just in case I was labouring under some deluded misapprehension, I was forcibly reminded never to "bring into the library, or kindle therein, any fire or flame". I took solace from the fact that I hadn't been singled out to make such a public commitment. This was normal procedure. In fact, once I'd cast my first superficial glances at the priceless collections housed inside this magnificent building I understood their need to take every precaution.

British libraries normally allow members to loan books for different periods, but uniquely the Bodleian is replete with reference materials so that all its papers and volumes must be read within the dedicated reading rooms. Furthermore, it is usual to order the manuscripts in advance. Depending on the exact location of the material required, it could take between 30 minutes and 24 hours to recover some crucial document from the innermost recesses of this extraordinary place.

This time delay was especially in evidence one day while I was waiting patiently inside to meet a colleague. I was sitting minding my own business in the reception area near to the main desk where two librarians were preoccupied in a joint enterprise of some sort. After a while, the mind-stirring peacefulness of the scene was rudely punctured by a shrill telephone ring. One of the pair immediately answered it and, after a few monosyllabic replies, replaced the receiver before recording a short note on a pad closeby. At this point, he turned to his colleague and muttered unceremoniously: "We'll have to be quick with this one." He passed across what I took to be a book request. Then, with the same inscrutable gaze he added even more dryly, "That was Roger Bannister on the phone and it won't take him long to get here." The Bodleian had been in existence since 1602 but I doubted it had ever borne witness to such a brilliantly pithy line.

My research was completed in 1997, and I was awarded a PhD the following year due mainly to the methods I had created for extracting box rules from neural networks and techniques for determining input parameter influences. I was then unemployed.

Fortunately a good friend, and sometime angling partner, Graham Wheldon, found me a position on the weekly publication *Raceform On Saturday* where I covered the *Ratings* and *Trainers to Follow* columns. I was also able to extend this to *Raceform Update* where I covered ante-post races, two-year-old ratings and sire analysis. This did spoil my enjoyment of the sport though. I used to watch as many races as possible as well as attend meetings but once I started tipping this ended. I could no longer watch races on a Saturday and would often not check the performance of my selections until Monday morning when it was well in the past.

Even though I had no financial involvement, watching a selection lose, especially if it ran poorly, would make me feel frustrated, annoyed and despondent and, of course, having to tip in every race run over the weekend meant that there were more losers than winners. I never could find a way to deal with these feelings, especially the thought that my advice may have cost others money when a horse failed to win.

Essentially, since leaving university for the third and final time, my income has come from writing books, columns for various papers and magazines, undertaking research for various betting syndicates, sales of ratings and software via the internet and occasionally covering the Speed Page for the ATR web site. Plus betting, of course, using a range of systems developed over several years, some of which are outlined in the following chapter.

Chapter Eleven

Some Other Systems to Consider

The aim of a system is to highlight an area of the betting market for which the price available does not fully account for the chance of success of the runner. While there are profitable methods which are based on widely available data, generally the more obscure the system, in terms of information used, the better it will perform. Obviously it still needs to retain a degree of logic, but if the rule is constructed with data not readily available to the betting public, such as a set of unpublished ratings or a unique form of pedigree analysis, then its chance of long-term success is significantly improved.

Several of the systems I use nowadays are ratings-based. I first started to create ratings in the late 1980s and initially targeted two-mile handicap chases even though I was not particularly in favour of weight-biased races. Part of the reasoning behind this choice of race type was that a two-mile handicap chase provides the sternest test of a racehorse. Naturally long-distance races will place a greater emphasis on stamina, but in order to win a race over the minimum trip the horse must be quick over the ground and able to jump efficiently at speed. In essence my theory was that these races test a runner's ability more thoroughly, therefore the better horses should prevail more often.

I was swayed in this view by other sports. Snooker, for example, was in my mind one of the most difficult sports to master, and from Joe Davis, on to Ray Reardon and then Steve Davis, the sport had been dominated by a small number of the best players for many decades. The gap between the best and middle-ranking performers is of less importance in sports where good fortune plays a greater role. But the ability gap in snooker determines the outcome of matches more frequently because "luck" plays such an insignificant role.

Obviously I could have used non-handicap two-mile chases instead since these exhibit the same characteristics as their weight-adjusted equivalents. However, compared to non-handicaps, a greater depth of form was available for handicap races which would help create a more reliable set of figures.

As well as placing the emphasis on speed this particular race distance attracted specialist runners. Over longer distances horses would often be stepping up from, say, 2m4f to three miles, and others would be dropping back in trip from 3m2f whereas, over the minimum trip, horses could only come back in distance and these would normally still have historical two-mile form. Obviously there were some well-known exceptions such as Desert Orchid and One Man, but these were remarkable horses and in the main the two-mile test, especially in the better contests, was dominated by runners who excelled at just this distance.

Creating a full set of handicap figures using just the formbook and pen and paper was not a realistic option. Instead I initially opted for a race-by-race approach, though I did also keep a separate record of the figures for the very best runners. For each two-mile handicap chase I would search the form pages of the *Racing Post* and identify the horse with the greatest degree of cross-over form with the other runners in the race. Normally this was a well-exposed horse which had previously raced against several of the horses he or she was taking on again in the contest I was examining. This horse would be assigned a rating of 100, regardless of ability.

The other runners would then be rated relative to this horse using a weight-for-distance scale of one pound per length. So if one of the opponents had beaten the 100-rated runner by two lengths off level weights and was re-opposing on 3lbs worse terms, he would be given a figure of 99. Naturally some runners could not be rated directly from the key horse so it was necessary to rate them through a third animal using the same approach.

If I had a rating for most of the runners and could justify omitting those without figures, I would examine the top-rated runner in detail, check the suitability of the going and then decide whether or not to bet. On some occasions it was not possible to rate more than just a few horses in a race in which case I would simply pass over the event in favour of a different contest.

This approach worked well and I thought I could easily extend it to juvenile races run on the flat. However, while there were fewer races to rate, finding the necessary depth of collateral form was much more difficult and I soon realised that I needed to adopt a speed-figure based method for this race type.

Once I had established a method for calculating speed ratings for two-year-olds, I implemented it using a spreadsheet and tested it for just over a year. It worked well so I decided to extend it to cover all races, covering both codes. However there were simply too many races to continue with the manual calculation. Consequently I trained a set of neural networks to emulate the process and was then able to rate every horse that ran in Great Britain and Ireland, as well as a small selection of the top races in France in a relatively straightforward way.

What surprised me most about the speed figures was that they were very profitable for jumps races. I had expected that all-weather racing would provide the most suitable domain for these figures due to the consistency of the racing surface, but over the years, in terms of profit, turf juvenile two-year-old races have produced the best figures followed closely by jumps races, then all-weather contests and finally non-juvenile turf races. I now believe this is due to the levels of competition within the race types, with the non-juvenile handicap turf races being the most competitive and hence least profitable.

Ability ratings such as these can be a very useful component in a system. Unlike *Timeform* and *Racing Post* ratings, if you generate your own figures then they are unique and not known to the betting public. If they are accurate then they become very helpful. While there will be a significant agreement between the sets of figures from different sources, as there should be because they are all trying to measure the same attribute of a runner, when there are differences there exist opportunities for making a profit.

For horses which have raced several times there will be a set of ratings associated with their performances. For example, a colt which has run three times may have the following figures: 23, 65, 75, in race order. This runner is clearly improving having raised his rating from 23 on his first start to 75 for his last run. But in order to compare this runner with his opponents, it is necessary to convert this set of historical figures into a single master rating. Methods for doing this vary markedly and different approaches can be used depending on the race type. For instance, one method can be adopted for jumps ratings but an alternative approach could be used for ratings recorded for two-year-old contests.

The easiest method is to take simply the best rating the horse has achieved within a specific number of races or time period. In essence this approach assumes the horse is capable of repeating the best figure it ran to during this period. From the tests I have performed I would use this method for form ratings rather than speed figures. Due to their method of calculation form ratings are generally more consistent than speed figures which can vary significantly from race to race simply due to the pace of the event and the speed at which other races on the card are run. This can give rise to figures which are inflated and are very unlikely to be repeated by the horse. Therefore I would employ a method that, to some degree, averages the speed ratings to create a master figure.

Taking the simple arithmetic average of the last three or so non-zero ratings may work, but this places the same importance on each of the figures. For the previous example the average is 54 to the nearest whole number which would appear to be far too low. The horse has already run to a 75 and, if that was an outlier, then there is a 65 to support it which would suggest the true ability of the horse is at least 65 and probably somewhat higher. However, had the ratings been in the reverse order and were suggesting that the horse was deteriorating, then a figure of 54 would be reasonable and could easily be justified. This implies that the order is important when forming the master figure and that any averaging process should take this into account.

The most straightforward way is to implement a weighted average. Each non-zero rating is assigned a weight determined by its order. This weight is multiplied by the rating and the aggregate calculated. The total is then divided by the sum of the weights:

$$\text{Master Figure} = \frac{(\text{Rating}_1 * \text{Weight}_1 + \ldots + \text{Rating}_n * \text{Weight}_n)}{(\text{Sum of the weights})}$$

The weights can be chosen by the ratings compiler and will vary in size. For example the following weights could be used. These gradually reduce the influence of each rating in the series with the most recent making the greatest contribution:

1, 1/2, 1/3, 1/4 ...1/n

For our previous example these weights would give the following Master Figure:

$$\text{Master Figure} = \frac{(1*75 + 0.5*65 + 0.33*23)}{(1 + 0.5 + 0.33)} = 63$$

This seems to be a better estimate of the runner's true ability, though still on the low side. It is better in this case than the simple arithmetic mean and does illustrate how the weights affect the calculation. Furthermore, with this approach there is no need to limit the number of ratings used in the calculation. All non-zero figures can be used since the older they are the less impact they have on the master figure.

Naturally there are many combinations of weights that can be employed and they depend on how important the latest rating is thought to be. For example the weights:

1, 1/2, 1/4, 1/8, 1/16...

could be used if there was evidence to suggest that the more recent ratings are far more relevant than historical figures. Applying these weights to the previous example produces a master figure of 65, and for the reverse of the figures the master rating is 42.

One handicapper I know uses the Fibonacci sequence to define the weights for the calculation of the master rating. At first this may seem totally abstract and completely divorced from horseracing. Why would a mathematical series, albeit a well-known one, have any relevance to the calculation of racehorse ability ratings?

The Fibonacci sequence was named after Leonardo of Pisa, the Italian mathematician of the Middle Ages, who was also known as Fibonacci. As well as being an interesting mathematical diversion, the Fibonacci sequence has many practical applications in the fields of computing and music. The first few terms of the sequence are given below:

1, 1, 2, 3, 5, 8, 13, 21, 34, 55,...

Calculating any term in the sequence is straightforward and simply requires the addition of the two previous terms, so the next term in the series given previously is:

$34+55 = 89$

Mathematics is often referred to as the language of science and nature and this description is no more apt than when applied to the Fibonacci sequence. This simple list of numbers is apparent throughout nature from the fruitlets on a pineapple, and petals on flowers, to the structure of the Nautilus sea shell and the spiral pattern on a pine cone.

Given these properties the Handicapper decided to test it with his ratings and found that it worked well. He uses the last six figures, providing they were recorded within a specific time period, and applies the weights as follows:

$$\text{Master Figure} = \frac{(Rtg_1/1 + Rtg_2/1 + Rtg_3/2 + Rtg_4/3 + Rtg_5/5 + Rtg_6/8)}{3.16}$$

where Rtg_1 is the latest rating and Rtg_6 the oldest.

These weights give the same degree of importance to the most recent pair of figures then reduce the influence of the remainder. I have tested this set of weights with my figures and it does not improve their predictability. However, they may well improve other handicappers' ratings.

Rather than randomly testing different weights hoping to stumble on the optimum series, a better approach is to analyse the figures and identify the most relevant weighting approach in a structured way. One method is to generate the ratings produced by runners for a fixed number of historical races, as well as the rating the horse achieved on its next start. It is then possible to use a statistical technique, such as a regression model, to establish how much each should influence the calculation of the master figure, so that the difference between this rating and the rating achieved is minimised.

Unfortunately, such techniques do require the forecasting variables to be independent, and in this case they are not since a correlation will probably exist between the figures a horse produces on its consecutive runs. Therefore the results will only provide a rough guide to the most appropriate weights but could still be used after modification and testing.

A better alternative is to model a neural network on the historical ratings and use the rating achieved as the target output. The network will minimise the error in a similar way the regression model does but it will not suffer any, deterioration in its accuracy due to the close relationship of the input variables (ie the historical ratings). Once trained, the weights linking the inputs to the output node of the network can then be extracted and used in the calculation of the master figure. For my turf figures the neural network suggested I should be using: 1, 1/3, 1/4. This shows that the latest rating is far more important than the other figures, three times as influential as the second most recent rating in fact.

Naturally there are many different ways to calculate the master rating and while the approaches discussed can be used to good effect with some sets of figures, their applicability does depend very much on the ratings themselves and the manner of their calculation. For instance, it may be productive to optimise the figures by race conditions. This entails placing more emphasis on the figures recorded under race conditions which are most similar to those which the horse is about to race on. So, for example, the rating of a horse that has been running on fast ground and now faces a soft-going test may be better derived from the runner's previous soft-ground figures. This approach is more complex but the previous weighting method is still applicable, providing the use of the race order is replaced with a measure of the similarity between historical and current race conditions. For a detailed explanation of this process please refer to *Horseracing: A Guide to Profitable Betting* published by Raceform in 2004.

Usually simply backing the top-rated horse at starting price with bookmakers or the exchanges will not return a long term profit. This applies to both form-based and time-based ratings. In fact there is no reason why these horses should make a profit. The ability rating simply determines the most likely winner of a race which is not necessarily the best bet in the race. A fairer assessment of a set of ratings is the win rate, not the profit. The top-rated horses should, in theory, win at a higher rate than the other runners, with the success ratio declining as the rank of the rating increases. If a set of ratings does not follow this pattern, then they are unlikely to make a worthwhile contribution to the race-analysis process.

Although ratings are not designed to return a profit, there are occasions when the top-rated runners will be worth following without including many additional filters. For example, the speed ratings I create for jumps racing have made a 6p/£ profit for all handicap races run in Great Britain since 2005. There have been poor years during the period, for instance the 2010/11 season returned a heavy loss, but the overall figure is positive using exchange prices recorded just before the official race time. However I have found that, in general, supplementing speed figures with some type of form-based assessment can significantly improve their effectiveness.

Normally I would use the official handicap ratings, but for handicap races this is no help since the figures would be normalised by the weight each horse carries. Consequently, for jumps handicap races, I combine the speed figure with a simpler measure of recent form, specifically the finishing position of the horse on its latest run; then analyse by race distance. Restricting bets to all top-rated horses in jumps handicaps which had made the frame on their latest start improves the profit to 8p/£.

The bulk of this profit came from races at up to 2m2f, which is not too unexpected given the form of the ratings and the fact that the top-rated runners in these shorter races have a success rate of over 17 per cent compared to 14.5 per cent for contests over further. These 1,232 runners made an average profit of 22p/£; the 2010/11 season was still poor though at 3p/£ (which would probably convert to a loss after commission), but the overall figures are encouraging with respect to the validity of this approach.

For all race distances, running style seems to be a better measure of form than finishing position and is certainly worth investigating with ratings from other sources. Top-rated horses using my speed figures in handicap chases and handicap hurdle races, which raced predominantly up with the pace on their latest run, made 10p/£ profit from over 5,000 bets. For the shorter races, up to 2m2f, this figure improved to 26p/£.

The fact that the combination of speed and form works well is evidenced further by novices' chases. For this race grade it is possible to use the official handicap ratings as the form component. Backing all runners top-rated on speed and by the BHA produces an excellent win rate of almost 40 per cent as would be expected, but this does not translate to a profit simply because these horses are generally under priced, even on the exchanges.

Instead a more general measure of the form of the runner is required. The aim is to identify good horses which may be better than their BHA rating implies, and eliminate those runners with overly inflated speed ratings. The rule I have used successfully for several seasons is to back the runners which are top-rated against the clock only if their BHA rating is 120 or higher. This approach has generated 193 winners from the last 500 bets (38 per cent success rate) and a level stake profit to exchange prices of 16p/£ before commission.

The value of these methods appears to be due to the

combination of speed and form, so there is no reason why it should not also work with other sets of speed ratings, such as those published on the ATR website, though figures which are less well known will perform better in the long run.

For the much more competitive all-age turf handicaps a slightly different strategy is required. The speed figures still form the basis of the system, and are supplemented by a form element in the same way as the jumps handicaps. However, these horses only win at a rate of about 18 per cent and return a loss to level stakes due to the larger field sizes and more competitive nature of the contests. Clearly an additional condition is required for races that are so difficult to solve.

The average success rate for all horses in these races is about nine per cent, and this is very stable for horses which have been off the track for eight days or more and only begins to deteriorate when the course absence exceeds 80 days. But, for those returning to racing within seven days of their last run, the success rate is 12 per cent, significantly higher than the norm. And for runners which made the frame on their last start this figure increases to 18 per cent. This is the group that the speed ratings should target. Isolating the top-rated runners from this subset reduces its size to approximately 110 per season, and of these roughly a quarter are successful, making a profit at industry starting price of 8p/£, which equates to 22p/£ at exchange prices before commission. This rule has made a consistent profit for the last five years and hopefully it will continue to do so.

Horses running after a significant change to their usual racing pattern are always worth noting. Those runners tackling handicap races for the first time were analysed earlier in this text, but a more significant change is the switch from racing on turf to the all-weather surface. From the following table it can be seen that these all-weather debutant runners lose heavily, which is not the ideal starting point.

ANALYSIS OF ALL NON-JUVENILE RUNNERS ON THEIR AW DEBUT

AW Race Type	Wins	Runs	Wins%	Profit*/£
Non-Handicap	443	4341	10%	-0.37
Handicap	257	2703	10%	-0.20
All Races	700	7044	10%	-0.31

* profit given to industry starting price

A loss of 31p/£ overall is exceptionally poor and would appear to suggest that there is little to be gained from analysing these horses. However, on further investigation, the loss of 20p/£ for handicap races can easily be reduced to just 6p/£ for the 1,188 horses that were rated 70 and higher by the BHA. This figure translates to 17p/£ profit at exchange prices recorded just before the official off time of the race. This in itself would appear to be a viable system but these 200 points profit were based on a few long-priced winners and as such the reliability of the method is uncertain at best. It does suggest though, that there may be a way to profit from these runners.

The normal course would now be to check the success rates by trainer to see if there are any stables worth following in these circumstances. However is there any reason why a trainer would have a significantly better performance on the all-weather surface than turf? Training methods may produce instances where this is the case but in general such patterns are more likely to be simple statistical anomalies rather than trends. It would be difficult to justify an approach based on such a tenuous connection.

Like humans, horses pass traits to their offspring. These traits may be with respect to appearance, temperament, or more importantly for the racing enthusiast, ability and preferences for specific racing conditions such as the distance and ground conditions. For instance, the offspring of some sires will not be seen to their best until they get to race over middle distances, and the progeny of others will only produce their best on soft going. In many cases these preferences mirror those of their sire. So a more profitable guide may be found in analyses of the runners' pedigrees.

A simple breakdown of win rates and profit and loss figures by sire will show those which have been worth following in the past. However such a list will probably be dominated by the better sires whose progeny perform above average on both types of surface. Good sires, with progeny that have good records on both surfaces, are unlikely to be helpful since the change will not produce an improved performance, and while these are of interest to analysts building more general forecasting models, for the system player they are not going to be as useful.

The aim is to find sires whose runners are likely to improve for the switch from turf to the all weather, essentially those sires whose progeny satisfy the following win rate rule:

AW Win Rate > Turf Win Rate

It is important to form this condition around win rates, rather than profit, because the objective of the rule is to identify a guide to likely improvement. Using profit instead of success rate introduces another variable, specifically the price, which may mask the underlying pattern which we are trying to establish.

Of the 3,307 all-weather debutant horses that failed this rule, only 318 won returning a level stake loss to industry starting price of 36p/£ (-20p/£ at exchange prices before commission); the 3,737 runners that satisfied the rule made a loss to industry starting price of 13p/£ which equated to a profit of 1p/£ on the exchanges. These are not the most encouraging results, but it is worth noting that 70 per cent of the loss for all-weather debut runners is recorded by those starting at a price longer than 20/1, and this increases to 76 per cent for those meeting the above win rate rule. Removing these and focussing on the runners at the front of the market produces the following figures:

ANALYSIS OF ALL NON-JUVENILE RUNNERS ON THEIR AW DEBUT PRICED AT 20/1 OR LOWER WHICH SATISFY THE WIN RATE RULE

AW Race Type	Wins	Runs	Wins%	Profit*/£
Non-Handicap	223	1077	21%	0.00
Handicap	130	879	15%	0.00
All Races	353	1956	18%	0.00

* profit given to industry starting price

So the method breaks even to industry starting price which is equivalent to a 17p/£ profit on the exchanges before commission. A breakdown by year shows a reasonably uniform pattern with the exchange profit varying from 15p/£ to 21p/£, but an analysis by horse gender shows the profit increasing to 25p/£ for colts and geldings, and dropping to just 3p/£ for fillies and mares.

This is a reflection of the overall success rates by these two groups; colts and geldings won at a rate 33 per cent higher than their female opponents. Since the system is based on pedigree and the passing of traits between the sire and his offspring, omitting fillies could be justified, though this does reduce the sample size making the method less reliable. So in this instance I would be prepared to use the more general rule until I could be more confident about introducing a gender condition.

Chapter Twelve

End of the Road?

An important issue that needs considering prior to implementing any system is bet placement. Historically a bettor's choice was limited to betting on course or with a handful of high street bookmakers. For the majority of non-handicap races early prices were simply not offered and punters had to take either starting price or the odds on offer just a few minutes before the start of the race. This has completely changed in recent years due mainly to the increased popularity of the internet. All races are now priced up by many firms early in the morning, and by lunchtime all bookmakers will be offering odds for every race. Furthermore, racing enthusiasts can also bet on the exchanges. Obviously this can, to a certain extent, complicate the process of placing a bet, but it does offer many opportunities and bettors are now much better served as a result of the increased options.

Throughout this text, systems have been analysed by industry starting price and exchange prices, and invariably the profit and loss figures based on the exchange odds are more in the bettors' favour. This is in part due to the differences in the over-round associated with each runner. For prices offered by bookmakers this is generally between one per cent and two per cent per horse, but for the exchange prices the over-round for the whole race will rarely exceed one per cent at off time. This would seem to imply that simply betting on the exchanges is the most sensible course of action. However, this is not always the case. While an event with a low over-round offers a more attractive betting opportunity, the critical figure is the price offered about the race winner. So, although one betting medium may offer prices to a much lower over-round, it is not necessarily the best betting option. Though the following example is artificial in its form, it does illustrate the point about relative price structures.

I have ten unbiased coins on a table. My intention is to flip each one in turn and record the number of "heads". To make it more interesting two sets of prices are offered about the outcomes, which do you think offers the best value?

THE TEN COIN FLIP TEST

Number of Heads	Price Set A	Price Set B
0,1,2,3	4/1	19/4
4,5,6	8/15	1/2
7,8	4/1	5/1
9,10	33/1	90/1
Over-round	108%	102%

At first look it would appear that Price Set B offers the best betting opportunities simply because of the lower over-round. However, the most likely winning combination is the "4,5,6" group, which in fact should be successful at least

65 per cent of the time. By betting this choice with Price Set A, you are guaranteed to make a long-term profit, but not so with Price Set B nor any other option, since these would all result in a level stake loss over a period of time.

Fortunately horseracing is not artificial so prices and winning chances vary from race to race, but if one company is constantly offering lower prices about the winners, by utilising a more intelligent approach to pricing, then the over-round is irrelevant. It is dangerous to assume that given their lower over-round exchange prices offer the best value. In fact I have some systems which have returned a profit of between ten per cent and 15 per cent over the last few years at bookmakers' early prices, but have made a loss on the exchanges simply because the value is eroded during the day as the market becomes more efficient.

Of course you should always take the best price available and as a rule I would recommend first taking prices with bookmakers early in the day; if that is not practical then betting with the exchanges at off time is the next best option. Betting with bookmakers near to the off time, into the Tote pool, or at starting price is simply not a way to make a profit, and if this is your only option then I would recommend that stake money is used to purchase premium bonds instead.

Choosing the correct betting option is another area where the live test of a system can be invaluable. While implementing this final phase of system development, it is informative to record prices from various sources such as early bookmakers' odds, early exchange prices and off time exchange prices. However it is also necessary to note the price adjustments in the form of Rule 4 deductions which could apply to early prices, as well as making a note of the liquidity for the exchange prices and remembering to deduct the commission.

Taking early prices with bookmakers is likely to be the best approach, providing the structure of the system allows for this method of betting. However, if successful, then it will result in the account being closed. This used to happen years ago mainly for big-staking punters, but nowadays it appears that no matter how small the stake, if an account is in profit after a period of time, then it will either be restricted or closed.

I had high hopes that Bet365 would not be the same as many of the other firms, after all their television advertisement stated: "Keep backing those winners and we'll keep giving you free bets." But unfortunately I misjudged them and I now feel extremely disappointed that I recommended and promoted this firm via my website. My current maximum stake on a 5/2 shot is now £4. I did keep to my side of the bargain by "backing winners", but unfortunately Bet365 were not keen to accept my bets and effectively stopped me betting with them by imposing such severe restrictions. Bet365 may not act in a manner that would be considered acceptable in all other areas of retail but unfortunately they are not alone in that respect.

I placed my first bet with BetFred on my birthday, 23 May 2008. I placed my last bet on 22 May 2009. It was not my decision to stop betting, BetFred suddenly imposed a limit on my account and I was unable to get more than £10-£20 on a horse and on occasions the maximum allowable stake was literally just a few pence. This surprised me because during the 12 months I had been betting with them my maximum stake was only £40 and over the year I had placed a total of just £5,425. Very rarely did I back each way with over 98 per cent of bets placed as win singles. My profit during the year was only eight per cent (£428), yet I was deemed to hold an account they could not afford to retain, hence the restrictions. So the next time you see Fred Done's grinning face on an advertisement remember that BetFred is a firm that is not prepared to lose £400 to a punter over the course of a year regardless of the claims its owner may make in the press.

The only way I can describe the conduct of Victor Chandler bookmakers is extremely disappointing. I opened an account with "The Gentleman Bookmaker" in the late spring and over the summer placed a few £20-£50 system-based bets each day. My profit rose to a mere £3,000 then on the 25 September, less than four months since the date of opening, my account was closed. Customer services at VCBet said they did not have to give a reason for closing my account and they wouldn't!

In a TV interview Chandler once said that bookmaking is all about making a book, and making sure it is balanced in your favour which is why he does not close accounts of winning punters. It seems as if his opinion has changed. Though you may hear him on TV talking about accepting four- and five-figure bets this bookmaker, who was once described by the *Racing Post* as "arguably the most famous bookmaker in the world ... the Indiana Jones of bookmaking, the fearless, swashbuckling rails layer who lit up Britain's racecourses for two decades", is not prepared to accept even the smallest bets from some bettors if there is the suspicion that their accounts may remain in profit.

In order to replace my lost Victor Chandler account I opened one with Stan James, my local bookmaker. Exactly 30 days after opening the account I received an email listing the restrictions that had been placed on it. When I queried this I was initially told it was because my account was in profit; then, after another email, the excuse changed to "your bets tend to be arbs". By this they meant, I believe, that I was backing horses with them and then laying the bet off on the exchanges. Naturally this is utter nonsense since I never place lay bets and in fact I feel that it is not in the best interest of the sport for punters to be allowed to back horses to lose.

I have since been contacted by several punters who have received the same email, some even offered to submit their exchange account statements to prove they were not "arbing" but these offers were, of course, turned down by Stan James. Apparently this accusation by bookmakers is the standard excuse they give as a reason for account closure or restriction.

During my 30 days with them I had won, but not a great deal, just £2,500, and my maximum stake was just £40.

I had been betting with Boylesports for just over a year without any problems. However, on the first day of Royal Ascot things changed: I tried to place my usual £50 bets online, but was restricted to just £1.80 on a 5/1 shot. This was the day another punter allegedly placed £40,000 on Goldikova at 7/4. I was instructed by customer services that I had to place bets by telephone. This worked for a while but was very time consuming for me and their staff since every bet had to be authorised by the "trading team". To test this, during the Royal meeting I tried to place a £20 bet on a 2/1 shot, and even though they were busy I had to wait while the bet was authorised by the traders. This was for a bet with a £40 liability on a day when they would deal in millions. The pattern continued so I contacted customer services and explained that they were making other customers wait simply to authorise very small bets from me, I also contacted the chief executive officer. The result of this was further restrictions placed on my account, and in the end it became unusable.

Of the "Big Three" bookmakers Coral are undoubtedly the most fearful of losing even very small amounts. Over a four-year period I made just £1,500 profit on my Coral account mainly because it was very restricted at an early stage with all bets referred to the traders. The end came when referring bets was replaced by setting my maximum stake to £0.

Shortly after this my account was closed. From a bookmaker who claims to be a major player this was a surprising action given the small amount of money involved and possibly illustrates their intention to either convert their clients to the more lucrative casino games or simply prevent them betting on events where there remains a chance of long term profit.

If bookmaking is still based on creating a book, and the firms are prepared to accept a fixed amount, up to say £500, on a horse at its current price then I am not sure why an ever increasing number of punters are not allowed to have part of the bet when others are. This appears to me to be a case of discrimination. It is rather like waiting at the checkout of a large supermarket with a tin of beans only to be told by the shop's employee that you are not allowed to purchase the item whilst selling the same product to other shoppers without query. I feel that the BHA should make a condition of the Betting Licence that such discriminatory practices are not permitted and not allow Bookmakers to use these methods to make up for the failings of their own trading and pricing systems. After all, if new punters are to be encouraged to bet on horseraces they need to know that there is a possibility of success otherwise they will drift away from racing into other areas of gambling. If, after spending a great deal of time studying the sport and developing methods, these new recruits are simply not allowed to bet then it will dissuade others from taking an interest and the main basis for the existence of racing will be seriously undermined.

Fortunately a couple of Bookmakers, with whom I have held accounts for many years, will still accept my bets. Consequently I am able to continue betting, but only just, and in a very restricted fashion.

There are clearly a variety of motives for betting on the outcomes of horse races. I understand that, for some people, it is purely a pleasant pastime. These "occasion hunters" meticulously plan a day in the glorious outdoors in the company of some majestic, four-legged beasts and a tent or two stacked with an equally attractive range of optics. Their idea of winning is derived from the simple pleasure of just being there – ideally at a famous, sporting venue about which they can later boast, hoping against hope perhaps to be in the presence of kindred spirits of the celebrity kind. Other participants I have noted along the way, are essentially the thrill-seekers. Armed with a stash of notes they are slaves to the chase of the elusive windfall. They desperately seek to inject an average, mundane Monday with an adrenalin-filled half-hour or more. For them, racing is a form of escape, a transient diversion from the laborious predictability of daily routine.

Others bet purely for profit. Their aim is simply to accrue as much money as possible. These are calculating, deliberate, discriminating bettors who are selective in their methods. System players can largely be found in this last group although they have been known to try to beat the book with an occasionally more intuitive approach.

One common factor among system-users is their tendency to adopt a more long-term strategy. Backing the winner of a race is equivalent to a miner in mid-19th century California happening upon a small, golden nugget in a clear, mountain stream. It's an extremely welcome bonus but it's not strictly the aim. For systems' enthusiasts the objective is always to apply a method that locates the seam of gold itself and systematically exposes and extracts it over the subsequent months and years.

I bet alongside two other system players. We exchange information, such as ratings and pace figures as well as comparing the strengths and shortfalls of each others' profitable systems. One of these betting partners is driven purely by the desire to make personal profit, and duly makes an excellent living from the sport.

The other takes a completely opposite view. His primary motive for betting is based on a deep-seated commitment to aid the redistribution of wealth. He is a firm believer in this principle and consistently rejoices in relieving the bookmakers of their cash, using commission agents to actually place the bets before distributing the profit to worthy charities. In fact, he spends as much time researching the credentials of the charities, to which he donates so generously, as he does to the betting systems which govern his success rate. Last year for example, he made a total profit of £141,000. Of this he retained a mere £12,000 for his living costs and gave away the remaining £129,000 to good causes. Each is certainly a remarkable character and I admire them both immensely but my influences are different again.

My own driving force does not revolve entirely around profit-making. For me, the fundamental inspiration centres on an academic fascination. Essentially, I am dedicated to the discovery of the next winning formula. Once a path to achieving this is beginning to emerge, my mind is diverted towards the next challenge. Every solution is quite distinct and the assiduous deconstruction of each and every obstacle to the next success, is effectively my lifeblood.

It's a kind of restless devotion based around an underlying ritual: the initial idea; analysis of the data in detail; the development of a tested, justifiable system; and the eventual confirmation of the anticipated results over a period of time. All together, it represents a cyclical journey which is profoundly satisfying in a number of respects but especially on an intellectual level. It seems to feed a hunger in me that I can never quite satisfy, no matter how much I surrender to its charms. For some readers of these lines, it might approximate to solving a difficult problem in a tough, time-framed examination, or completing a challenging crossword or unravelling a tortuous logic puzzle. It's something to do with having to overcome a seemingly endless succession of baffling barriers. It is, in effect, like tackling a virtual steeplechase of my own invention, where your spirits and not your bones are jeopardised by the occasional fall.

I'd be mangling the truth to say I hadn't ever nearly lost

track of it all but the quest itself has been riveting – more so than the money. Mind you, when things click into place, the financial dividend is undoubtedly the cherry on my cake – the vindication, if you like, of all the mental energy that's been spent. The substantial part of the treat, though, derives from the act of unearthing that single, obscure feature of racing which produces another unique system and the promise of several seasons of solid success. The beauty of knowing that the brain's functioned on the back of a load of sheer graft is the thing I find most gratifying. It's a compelling cocktail if ever there was one and an irresistible one at that as far as I am concerned.

For many racing enthusiasts, reaching the end of the betting rainbow might mean the prospect of escaping a tiresome, nine-to-five existence. This was certainly, at one time, an uppermost consideration of mine, which I remember used to motivate me powerfully about 20 years ago. To a certain extent I have realised that goal, but to this day I still rely on other revenue streams apart from my most favoured one in order to supplement my income. It's a cautionary tip that anyone starting out from a similar position to myself should initially just aim to use betting profits to bolster existing earnings as opposed to strictly trying to replace them. The risks are too severe. From my point of view, a reliable income provides a safety net should the betting route eventually not prove as profitable as I'd first dared to hope.

In fact, I understand that voluntarily giving up paid

employment to immerse oneself in a full-time, full-on battle with the bookmakers has been known to result in a range of unexpected, psychological impacts. If the bet selection methods are based purely on race analysis techniques, then it is possible that the bettor will become more conservative in his approach with a consequent risk to profitability. This is a natural response to new working conditions and it is essential for any current or would-be bettor to identify such a change. Monitoring the actual frequency of bets placed will help to demonstrate whether an individual's betting inclinations have been reduced or not, but making the necessary changes required to avoid this tendency may not be so straightforward.

For system players this is not such a problem, since the bets are generated automatically, but a protracted losing run is likely to engender that same level of reserve. In these circumstances tried and tested systems become the objects of tinkering efforts to rectify the situation. Longer term losses are often dictated by such short-term meddling with proven methods. All in all, as a stand-alone business model, system betting is insecure enough to warrant the retention of that additional source of income, just to tide the bettor over during the inevitable stickier times.

Where betting is found to be the sole source of earning it is safe to assume that higher stakes are in play, especially in cases where it is replacing a once substantial salary. On the one hand, hugely increasing stakes can produce significantly higher returns, but on the other, it can make the betting itself more difficult if profits are slow to accumulate.

As I've suggested already, absolute profit is not my main aim, and therefore I'm content to speculate with relatively small stakes with which it's still possible to generate a reasonable profit. Placing 40 to 60 bets per day takes my turnover for the year past the half a million pounds mark, so an average profit per bet of just five per cent generates a fair return for the sizeable effort involved.

This, in effect, is my salary and I'm comfortable with it. However, the average profit figure remains critical to me. Even if this is a minor, negative figure over a significant period of time then I can become quite disillusioned with the systems, a state of mind that can sometimes extend to an actual aversion towards betting in general during a particularly poor run. Naturally, if I had a more regular job, I could use it to distract my attention during these leaner spells, but when work and hobby are synonymous it is more difficult to dismiss setbacks and the mood duly suffers for a while.

Working from home is another factor which is bound to have a determining influence on that sense of well-being. Years ago, my first thought was that a life unencumbered by the grind of the daily, office-commute, was extremely appealing. However, the reality, as is often the case in life, has not always felt as glamorous as my original anticipation had persuaded me. Switching at once from the constant human interactions of an office environment to a day-upon-day existence in near isolation is something to consider very carefully before adopting this new lifestyle.

The absence of a work-related social life can, for many people, make this new, yet very familiar, working environment a distinctly lonely place. While seemingly a trivial point, it should not be underestimated since studies have shown that such circumstances have resulted in many cases of severe depression. Some people are well suited to working from home and I consider myself among them but I have experienced such moments and had to overcome them. It's simply a price to be paid and I have learned to accept it.

The working day itself for a full-time gambler tends to be much longer than average and of course includes weekends. Sacrosanct time to call one's own is often in short supply. While this is not necessarily a significant problem to the gambler himself, in charge of his own immediate destiny and understanding completely the reasons for its all-consuming demands, it can cause some understandable resentment and agitation on the part of other family members whose needs are too often sacrificed at the altar of fickle betting ambitions.

Fortunately, in terms of my being able to enjoy enough time and space for my own work, my wife is a dedicated teacher so her own school-related commitments usually stretch well beyond 10pm each evening, and sometimes much later into the night. Such are the expectations these days levelled at those doing their utmost to educate the next generation, she is also required to dedicate vast slices of the weekend to her pupil's needs. All this being so, my often unsociable working hours haven't created as much tension as they might have and luckily our enforced mutual absences have, on the whole, not caused too many problems.

The plain fact is that the lifestyle also requires a strong and understanding partner in the background, whose devotion to the gambler and any children involved, is equal to his necessary obsession with the system. For me to have survived in the game without Sara is unlikely; to have succeeded to the extent I have, simply inconceivable.

I have now enjoyed working from home for over ten years, and although there have been times when I considered reverting to conventional employment, I no longer see this as a viable option. In spite of all the aforementioned drawbacks, I too highly prize my freedom. The very thought of labouring under constraints imposed by an unsympathetic employer is enough to make me wince. Juggling 40 hours per week in an office for a further decade or two would force me to abandon everything else I've grown to love about the fortunate life I lead. The compromise would be huge and the prospect fills me with a deep sense of dread.

A professional punter once said to me, "Betting is the best way to make a living there is." I would personally qualify that by adding, "For some people – not everyone." Certainly, it promises an exciting alternative to more ordinary ways of making a living and is the perfect occupation for risk-takers of a certain kind. The chances of the whimsical, spur-of-the-moment, bounty hunter would nosedive very quickly, but for the measured, detailed-thinker whose application remains unfazed after relentless hours of often unrewarded toil, it's the perfect match.

It's useful, too, to be mindful of having to face the wearing criticism of those detractors who feel that such a career path makes no worthwhile contribution to society. Unlike jobs in medicine or education which have obvious benefits to the population in general, betting is simply a matter of shifting money from one place to another. But in this respect it is the same as many thousands of pen-pushing and paper-shuffling jobs which merely facilitate the transfer of wealth from clients to company directors and shareholders.

Even so, my conscience would probably be pricked more painfully if I felt that betting was my only cause. Freely designing software for assessment systems in schools, publishing daily ratings and writing books and articles of different sorts, all to a lesser or greater extent, help me feel I'm able to have some beneficial impact on at least a few others. I like to feel that what I do outside of betting constitutes the provision of some sort of minor, public service and one that compensates (in limited style admittedly) for the fact that my time is chiefly exhausted by largely self-serving actions.

If all this seems like some sort of self-justification, that's exactly what it is. I'm quite prepared to confess it. But the point is that without a sense of achieving something reasonably close to a natural balance in commitments, I would be unable to continue as I have been doing much longer. As it stands, I foresee my working ways being very similar for a good few years to come. While the thought of remaining forever home-based might one day have me knocking on the psychiatrist's front door, the search for the bespoke winning system is one that continues to propel me from day to day in a kind of pot-of-gold pilgrimage, constantly combating the ever-changing betting environment in the most intriguing, academic marathon anyone could wish to run.

Index